IMAGES
of America

JAPANESE AMERICANS OF FLORIN

I0802380

A number of contributors, including Mary and Al Tsukamoto, collaborated to map out the location of Florin's Japanese American farms prior to 1942 exclusion. This is a small section of the impressive map, which covers not only Florin but also its adjacent agricultural regions. (Courtesy of the California State University, Sacramento, Japanese American Archival Collection.)

On the Cover: Nami Miyata stands with her youngest son, Ted Miyata, in a Florin strawberry field on George Tanaka's ranch on May 11, 1942. A widow since 1921, Nami Miyata raised six children and for a time made a living working in a Florin basket factory until three acres of strawberries were leased by her children. Japanese American military members were furloughed in order to come home and help their families prepare for forced removal and years-long detention mandated by Executive Order 9066. (Photograph by Dorothea Lange, courtesy of US National Archives and Records Administration.)

IMAGES
of America

Japanese Americans of Florin

Michelle Trujillo
Foreword by Marielle Bliss Tsukamoto

ARCADIA
PUBLISHING

Copyright © 2020 by Michelle Trujillo
ISBN 978-1-4671-0591-0

Published by Arcadia Publishing
Charleston, South Carolina

Printed in the United States of America

Library of Congress Control Number: 2020939647

For all general information, please contact Arcadia Publishing:
Telephone 843-853-2070
Fax 843-853-0044
E-mail sales@arcadiapublishing.com
For customer service and orders:
Toll-Free 1-888-313-2665

Visit us on the Internet at www.arcadiapublishing.com

This book is dedicated to the memory of Issei trailblazers and society's "others." Whether conspicuous or invisible, your everyday persistence is nothing short of revolutionary.

Contents

Foreword

Florin was a small rural town nine miles south of Sacramento originally settled by early pioneers traveling west on the new transcontinental railroads. In 1875, the town was officially named Florin for the beautiful flora in the surrounding fields. The year 1890 brought the first immigrants from Japan, who came seeking the American dream: opportunity, liberty, and a better life for their American-born children. These innovative farmers raised two crops, strawberries and grapes, doubling their income.

Florin grew and flourished. Businesses and shops were built next to the original stores; Buddhist and Christian churches became the centers of the Japanese community. By 1941, ninety percent of the residents were Japanese. They expected the best crop ever and many anticipated paying off mortgages and other debts. The war ended these dreams, especially for the Americans of Japanese ancestry and their immigrant parents (labeled enemy aliens). Pres. Franklin Roosevelt's Executive Order 9066 allowed Gen. John DeWitt to impose martial law on the West Coast and the forced removal and imprisonment of all persons of Japanese ancestry.

The entire community of Americans of Japanese ancestry was forced to leave homes, farms, and businesses and was sent to concentration camps with only what they could carry. Florin became a shell of a town.

In 1945, these displaced Americans were allowed to return, but 85 percent had lost their property and livelihoods, and fires had destroyed most of the houses and businesses in town.

Today, Florin is a location on Florin Road.

The US Constitution provides for due process. In 1988, Pres. Ronald Reagan signed legislation authorizing an official letter of apology and $20,000 reparation for those still alive.

Thank you Michelle Trujillo for preserving the history of Florin, California.

—Marielle Bliss Tsukamoto

ACKNOWLEDGMENTS

This book is the result of my master of arts thesis project in public history from California State University, Sacramento (CSUS), with the assistance of a number of people, both directly and indirectly. The idea was presented to me by Julie Thomas, the instruction and electronic records archivist and steward of the Japanese American Archival Collection at the Gerth Special Collections and Archives at CSUS. Her steadfast support was critical in allowing me to submit my project on time. Julie holds a unique familiarity with the collection, and her belief in the importance of this project aligned with my sense of purpose in telling this part of Florin's Japanese American experience through photographic imagery.

Julie Thomas also connected me with Marielle Bliss Tsukamoto, who was four years old when her family was ordered by the US Army to leave Florin on May 29, 1942. Marielle Tsukamoto is a retired teacher but an active educator and Japanese American Citizens League member who continues to support her community and inform people about World War II Japanese American incarceration, including as a speaker at the California Museum in Sacramento. I'd like to thank Marielle for welcoming me to her home and taking time to share her stories, memories, and resources about Florin families and for helping me navigate the telling of sensitive family history. Mary Tsuruko (Dakuzaku) Tsukamoto, Marielle Tsukamoto's mother, never stopped teaching Japanese American World War II internment history and fought tirelessly for redress. Mary Tsukamoto's memoir, written with Elizabeth Pinkerton and titled *We the People: A Story of Internment in America*, contains some of the most poignant, damning, and beautiful passages regarding Japanese American exclusion and incarceration that I've read.

Thank you to Dr. Lee Simpson and Dr. Brendan Lindsay, my master's advisory committee, and my CSUS professors who have supported me throughout graduate school, wrote letters of reference, lent me materials, and encouraged me to step beyond my comfort zone and present my research. Your feedback and perspectives always provided a pathway for me to be a stronger researcher and writer, and the process shaped my voice as a public historian.

I give my deepest gratitude for my family's support and interest in this project. Finally, thank you to my wife for being unflappable, nurturing, honest, and funny. You have been my rock throughout the rollercoaster that is grad school and I'm so lucky to be going through life with you by my side.

Unless otherwise noted, all images appear courtesy of the Japanese American Archival Collection at California State University, Sacramento.

Introduction

The majority of the photographs in this book are housed at the Japanese American Archival Collection (JAAC). October 2019 marked the JAAC's 25th year after its beginnings as an educational partnership between California State University, Sacramento (CSUS), and the Florin Japanese American Citizens League (JACL). The collection includes oral histories donated by the Florin JACL, documents from the Sacramento Veterans of Foreign Wars Nisei Post 8985, and community donations, including most of the photographs in this book. Housed at CSUS's Gerth Special Collections and University Archives, the JAAC's creation was led by Florinite and "Notable Californian" Mary (Dakuzaku) Tsukamoto, an educator, speaker, author, and activist who was sent with her immediate and extended family to Japanese American concentration camps in Fresno, California, and Jerome, Arkansas, between 1942 and 1945.

The town of Florin was the business center of the surrounding region, but "Florin" was also used to collectively refer to its outlying areas: Taishoku, Mayhew, Brighton, Elder Creek, Perkins, Walsh Station, and California Vineyard. Elk Grove, incorporated in 2000, did not fall under the "Florin" designation and is the southernmost region documented in the archival photographs presented in this book. Elk Grove's train station was the setting for many of Florin's Japanese American departures due to forced removal and the location of the Wartime Civil Control Authority (WCCA) office, where Japanese American families were ordered to register prior to exclusion.

Florin came into its own, like so many California cities, with the arrival of the Central Pacific Railroad in 1870. When the town was founded in 1875, Florin already had 15 extant buildings including a saloon, box factory, general store, hotel, and blacksmith shop. The Florin railroad depot was an early link to a future that was abruptly severed with the onset of World War II, never to return to its role as the region's agricultural mainstay.

Today, the rural vestiges and suburban growth that characterize the unincorporated town of Florin both obscure and reveal its unique past. Florin is nine miles southeast of California's capital of Sacramento and near three critical rivers (the Sacramento, American, and Cosumnes) that continue to shape Sacramento's identity as the River City, its landscape, and its politics. Approximately 10 miles square, these "Highlands," as the area was known by the Miwok, have witnessed a transformation from hunting and ceremonial grounds of the indigenous Miwok and Nisenan peoples to fertile farmland for European Americans seeking a life beyond Gold Rush promises. The influx of European American farmers into Florin during the early to mid-19th century was the final push for Native Americans out of their sacred and subsistence lands. For Japanese community members, Florin stood as a crucible proving the limits of citizenship, capitalistic inclusion, and civil rights. Aided by anti-Japanese propaganda in newspapers, California's history of white supremacist organizations, public servants, and business owners stamped an everlasting mark on Florin's topography.

Japanese laborers proved to be an important element in California agriculture by the turn of the 20th century and were not regarded with mistrust as long as they remained in the laboring class. Japanese immigrants were drawn to Florin to fulfill its labor needs and created opportunities for themselves to transcend economic classification from laborer, to renter, to owner. The growing use of irrigation in the 1890s, combined with labor contractors pulling immigrant labor out of the cities and into canneries and farms, allowed for innovations and growth in local agriculture, specifically the specialization in strawberries and grapes. Japanese workers were willing to do the difficult stoop labor associated with these crops because the income from consistent harvests allowed them a stable opportunity to build new lives in Florin. In turn, growing demand for these sweet fruits crowned them as Florin's most popular crops. Continuing to predominantly produce fruit, Florin shipped its first trainload of strawberries in 1893.

Before Japanese innovations, Florin farmers managed only small returns on their crops using unrefined farming techniques, which limited growth to one harvest and achieved results hardly worth the effort. However, the difficult landscape was transformed into "productive and profitable fields, orchards, and vineyards for the Japanese who took over from them, and raised excellent crops," according to the April 30, 1913, *San Francisco Call*. In a *Pacific Rural Press* article, landowner Leonard M. Landsborough gave appropriate credit when he acknowledged that "the people [in Florin] did not make a success of strawberry culture until the advent of the Japanese." Despite the success of strawberry crops, anti-Japanese whites were on alert for opportunities to create obstacles to Japanese advancement and pledged to "wage with even greater energy the campaign which they [had] begun against the Japanese in [Florin]," reported the *Mariposa Gazette* on June 3, 1905.

What was special about Japanese strawberry cultivation techniques? One innovation included the use of narrow but deep ditches to retain moisture rather than the shallow ditches previously employed. They also devised a strategy of planting the rows of strawberries on an east-west axis to expose the plants to the sun for longer, which caused them to be weeded on an earlier timeline. Collectively, less shading and better moisture retention translated into continuously growing plants. This allowed for earlier harvests and was key to Florin's strawberries beating other regions' berries to market. Japanese farmers capitalized on the east-west orientation and the resulting early ripeness. The new successful techniques were such a boon for Florin that Landsborough acknowledged that even property values increased due to the creativity implemented by Japanese farmers.

From 1900 through 1910, Japanese farmers bought property and established their own profitable farms, while some did likewise through leasing. Florin's agricultural output increased the profitability of white land-owning enterprises leasing to Japanese farmers. Nonetheless, bigoted rhetoric characterized the Japanese agricultural industry as theft of American jobs and land, despite supporters' claims that their work was an integral contribution to California's food needs and economic expansion. By the 1910s, racist rhetoric helped produce legislation targeting Japanese immigrants in California.

The California legislature passed the 1913 Webb-Hartley Law (Alien Land Act) prohibiting land ownership or land leases longer than three years for "aliens ineligible to citizenship" and targeted Japanese immigrants because they were not allowed to naturalize under federal law. However, their children were born citizens and therefore could hold land in their names. The contention of the Alien Land Act spurred a debate among white Florin community members over which view represented the majority of the town, be it in support for or objection to land-owning rights for Japanese.

There were about 2,000 Japanese Americans in Florin in 1913. A 1923 survey showed seven-eighths of the population was Japanese; this proportion brought in and encouraged white agitators and opponents to Japanese advancement. The 1924 Immigration Act stopped most Japanese from coming to California, and the "banner of discrimination was waved openly in Florin," according to Mary Tsukamoto's memoir *We the People: A Story of Internment in America*. Still, a pervasive preoccupation among whites in California during the early 20th century was that "it was altogether likely that California's most difficult task would be to remain American in composition," according to Robert Heizer and Alan Almquist in *The Other Californians: Prejudice and Discrimination under Spain, Mexico, and the United States to 1920*. Gov. Hiram Johnson had roots in Florin as a young schoolboy and regardless of whether his scapegoating of Florin was rooted in nostalgia or "racism based on envy," in the words of Kevin Starr in *California: A History*, it is clear his motivations were to maintain California's whiteness.

Price fixing of labor costs, denial of land ownership, segregated schools, rejection of a burial ground, and exclusion from positions of authority all worked in concert to try and keep Japanese

Florinites marginalized and economically stunted. But Japanese farmers fought for their place by adopting a very American approach; that is, by interpreting existing laws to their advantage and pushing back against the injustices they faced.

By the time Japan bombed Pearl Harbor in 1941, Florin had established itself as the largest fresh strawberry shipper in the United States. Despite this clear evidence of long-term Japanese presence, integration, and economic- and community-bolstering success, the Pearl Harbor attack changed everything. Pres. Franklin Roosevelt signed Executive Order 9066 on February 19, 1942, which "authorized the U.S. Army to exclude populations from designated zones when deemed necessary for security reasons." The Army evacuated 122,000 men, women, and children of Japanese ancestry from their homes on the West Coast, displacing them from their businesses, pets, land, and most of their belongings.

Much like the Alien Land Act, Executive Order 9066 was written carefully to allow for discrimination of Japanese Americans, with a common understanding of its purpose: the US government's replacing of Japanese American farmers with "American" ones. Exclusion was not an anomaly for Japanese regarding land ownership, especially after the passage of the 1913 and 1920 Alien Land Acts, because marginalization and dehumanization had been an everyday occurrence in California for decades. But Japanese immigrants had sacrificed and organized for better wages enough to make forays beyond farm labor and into farm ownership and management, and this step into the capitalist class was a perceived threat to white farm operators. The arrival of World War II provided an unprecedented opportunity to reappropriate Japanese farming concerns—under the guise of the exigencies of war—by methodically plucking Japanese agricultural workers and their families out of their livelihoods, much like countless precious Florin strawberries had been, right from the stem.

Despite immigration restrictions, prohibitions of land ownership, and segregation, Japanese immigrants and their descendants established families and businesses in ways that exemplify American values. If not for their innovation and hard work, Florin's hardpan would have gotten the better of the town's white farmers. Instead, Japanese immigrant and Japanese American farmers launched Florin to strawberry supremacy, and in so doing also increased the wealth of Florin's white landowners. The culminating manifestation of decades of racist laws and everyday bigotry occurred with Executive Order 9066 in 1942, which opportunistically reappropriated hard-fought Japanese American livelihoods into the hands of majority white interests. Japanese American Florinites returned from World War II incarceration to a once-bustling farming town transformed into piecemeal fragments of their old lives that were either burned down, stolen, or neglected. The few fortunate families who had made arrangements with white friends tried to recover their businesses, but most gave up after a few years. Florin's landscape still holds clues to its agricultural past, though suburban sprawl continues its creep across the old farmlands. Florin's farming pedigree is less and less apparent when driving through today.

A note on terms: The language of World War II Japanese American incarceration—"internment," "relocation," "evacuation," "internment camp," and "relocation camp"—are beset by the words' euphemistic softening and distortion of the fact that the US government was stripping its citizens of their rights. This terminology was used by the government and military to sway public opinion about these actions. Beginning in the 1970s, historians and scholars studied the wartime vocabulary and concluded that updated word choices were necessary to accurately convey the exclusion and detention of people of Japanese descent from the West Coast. In 1945, the US Supreme Court determined that Japanese American detention was a violation of their constitutional rights. In 1983, the Commission for Wartime Relocation and Internment of Civilians (CWRIC) published a report titled *Personal Justice Denied* that concluded it was "race prejudice, war hysteria, and a failure of political leadership" that entitled Executive Order 9066 to pass, and not "military necessity." Following the recommendations of the CWRIC report, I use language such as "forced removal" instead of "evacuation" and "concentration camp," "detention center," and "incarceration camp" instead of "internment camp" or "relocation center." Quoted words identify euphemistic terms such as the Fresno "Assembly" Center or Jerome "Relocation" Center. For explanations of preferred language regarding Japanese American forced removal and detention, please visit JACL.org or Desho.org.

One

The Town of Florin

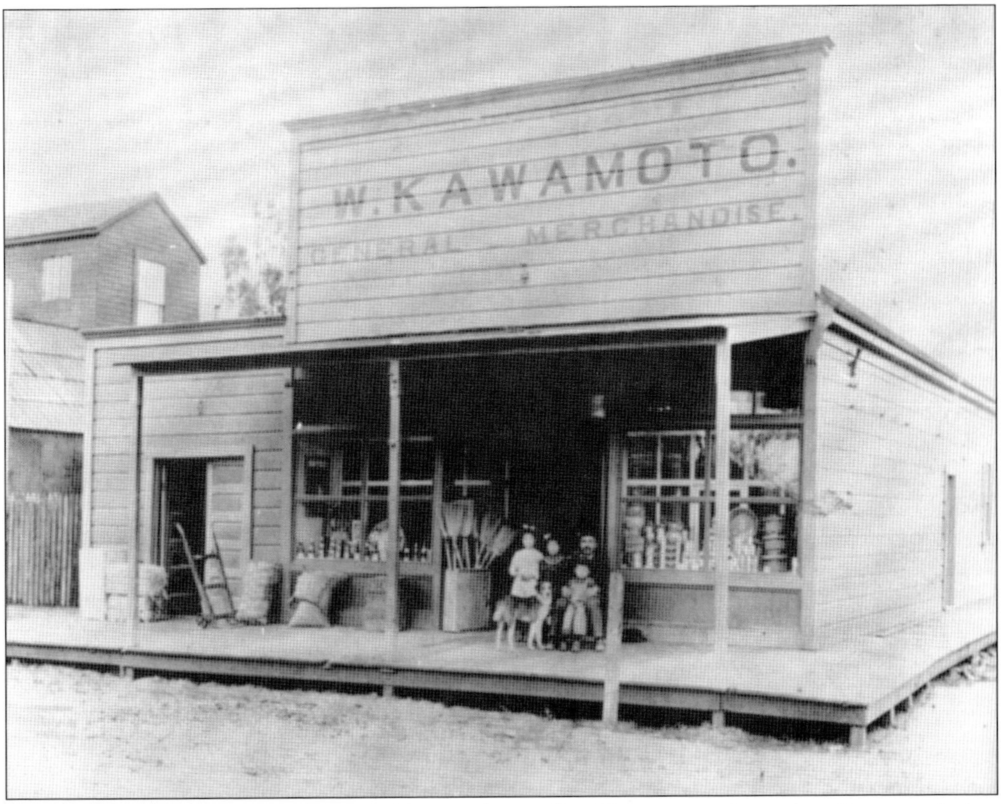

Wakichi Kawamoto poses with his children in front of his Florin general merchandise store during the early 1900s. From left to right are Chiyeko, Matsuko, Wakichi, and Takeo. Wakichi Kawamoto passed away in June 1910, and the business was eventually taken over by Tamazo Tanikawa, who also acquired the adjacent building that belonged to H. Kato. The store, at the corner of Reese and Florin Roads, burned down but was rebuilt and operated until the forced removal of Florin's Japanese American community in 1942.

The 1869 completion of the Central Pacific Railroad brought rail lines through Florin in 1870, with many stops at the Florin depot, shown in this undated photograph. By this time, the area was already a strong producer of fine fruits, grain, and hay, which allowed the community to prosper. The 1876 freight books marked Florin's agricultural productivity as 160,749 pounds of strawberries and blackberries, 182 tons of hay, 260 tons of grapes, and additional produce such as boxes of tomatoes, apples, pears, peaches, and onions.

A train has pulled into the Florin train depot in this c. 1920 photograph. The Florin Fruit Exchange and General Merchandise stands in the distance, visible by its large sign. Leonard Landsborough, a Florin landowner and former manager of the fruit exchange, assisted Japanese Issei (first generation) by purchasing land and putting the title in the names of their American-citizen children (Nisei). The money used to purchase the land came from Japanese families.

This c. 1932 photograph shows a view of Florin Road looking east over the railroad. A drive down this road would have led to many Japanese farms producing strawberries and grapes. Family farms would have included Kiyama, Inouye, Shigeno, Takayama, Horimoto, and Yoshimura. By 1924, seven-eighths of Florin's population was Japanese, and the 1942 forced removal decimated the town's economic and social frameworks.

The Florin Basket Factory, shown here around 1913, was managed by a Mr. Masuda, though Japanese workers were overseen by a white boss, as shown in the photograph. Japanese laborers packed grapes into baskets, which were then placed into crates. Most of the workers were men, because the few Japanese women who had arrived in Florin at this time tended to their farms and homes. Most of these women were known as picture brides, meaning the marriage was arranged by a matchmaker who exchanged photographs between the potential bride and groom. Japanese women arrived as picture brides for many different reasons, such as to fulfill familial obligations or achieve economic stability.

This c. 1915 scene is inside what was possibly Florin's first packing shed. Japanese Issei women sit at workstations, while a presumptive supervisor stands nearby. Abundant strawberry and grape production sustained Florin's economic stability for nearly 60 years, and this consistency allowed Japanese farmers to have families, buy land, and develop businesses.

Yaiichi Nishi is standing in front of a Seybold automatic paper-cutting machine at his Capital Basket Company in this c. 1920s photograph. An earlier map shows the location of an "old basket factory" as well as Yaiichi Nishi's basket factory, both of which were near Florin Road. Someone set fire to and destroyed Nishi's business shortly before he returned from detention in 1945.

Proper packaging was a mandatory component in Florin's high-volume strawberry production process, because it brought the fruit to market intact. This c. 1935 photograph shows workers at the Florin basket factory, each at their own similar workstation. Tall piles of basket slats indicate the continuous nature of the work.

Assigned as a War Relocation Authority (WRA) photographer to document Japanese American exclusion, Dorothea Lange photographed this woman and two little girls sitting in front of a Japanese-owned store in Florin. Forced removal was merely two days away when this 1942 picture was taken, so Florin families were in the midst of making hasty arrangements for their homes, businesses, and property. (Photograph by Dorothea Lange, courtesy of Densho.org.)

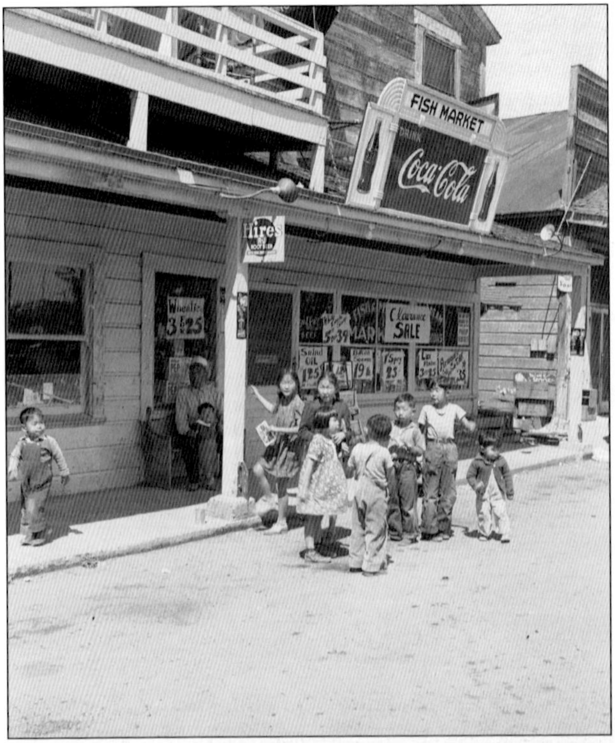

A group of children are congregated in front of H. Kato's fish market and grocery, which advertises Coca Cola, Wheaties, salad oil, lunch meat, and other sundries. A "Clearance Sale" sign hangs in the window in this 1942 photograph, taken two days before exclusion was to begin. Japanese Americans did not have the luxury of time to handle most of their personal affairs, and many were not fairly compensated for the belongings, land, cars, and farm machinery that they were forced to sell or store. Those who did return to Florin after incarceration camps were closed found major losses due to looting, vandalism, or theft by trustees without the owners' knowledge. Below, a child can be seen behind the screen door. (Both photographs by Dorothea Lange, courtesy of Densho.org.)

The town of Florin was the region's business district and catered to the community's varying consumer and business needs, including a fish market, barbershop, and midwife services. Behind the oak trees of this 1942 image is a water tower. The white parapet facade is Grey's Garage, and down the street to the left is a railroad crossing. (Photograph by Dorothea Lange, courtesy of Densho.org.)

Nakayama Shoe Repairing, shown here in 1942, was on the north side of Florin Road next to the Sasaki Tofu-ya (tofu shop). The Southern Pacific Railroad tracks sat to the west of Nakayama's along with a number of other businesses on this strip of Florin Road. (Photograph by Dorothea Lange, courtesy of Densho.org.)

Baseball player Herb Kurima (left) and "Mayor" Fuju Sasaki pose together in this undated photograph. Fuju and his wife, Kikue Sasaki, owned a tofu shop in Florin between the Southern Pacific Railroad tracks and McComber Street. Sasaki Tofu-ya was on the north side of Florin Road between Akiyama's grocery and Nakayama's shoe repair shop. "Mayor" was a term of endearment for this admired community member. Japanese exclusion forced the Sasakis to incarceration camps in Fresno and Jerome.

Two

A WAY OF LIFE

This portrait, taken between 1911 and 1916, shows Dr. Matsue Suzuki. In 1911, Dr. Suzuki was possibly the only doctor in Florin, and might have treated both Japanese and white patients. Her medical office was in the same building as Florin's barbershop, the site of a large group photograph of early Issei. Her practice could be located by a sign that translated as "Suzuki Medical Office." Dr. Suzuki earned her medical degree in Tokyo and after arriving in San Francisco studied at Lane Hospital for one year. Her husband was a former secretary of the Japanese Association of Florin.

The Florin Japanese Association is shown in 1916. Japanese associations supported and protected Japanese in business dealings and assisted with teaching American customs and culture. By 1913, a number of Japanese associations had been established in California, in Marysville, San Francisco, San Bernardino, and San Diego.

The Taisho Young Men's Association building frames the subjects of this c. 1940 photograph of members of the Young Men's and Young Women's Association in Florin. "Taishoku," an area settled by Japanese Issei near Florin, refers to Emperor Taisho, whose reign began around the time Taishoku was settled.

This 1911 group photograph of Florin's Issei was taken in front of a building that served as the barbershop and medical facility for Florin's Japanese American community. Much of daily life was segregated between Japanese and whites, such as barbershops, schools, sports teams, and churches. Identified here are Kuzo Tsukamoto (seated in front of the tree) and Ito Tsukamoto (seated fourth to the right of the tree). Tsumayo Kawamura and Kinuye Shiohama each established a midwifery practice, or *sanin*, next door to each other on Florin Road.

Japanese met strong resistance in Florin during the early 20th century in their search for a cemetery. When it came time for Japanese Florinites to petition the board of supervisors to establish a cemetery within the town boundary, whites counter-petitioned to deny them. An editorial reply commenting on the denial of a burial ground for Japanese community members stated, "Some towns will not let them live, but Florin would forbid them burial if they quit living. It's hard lines." The destination of this c. 1913 funeral procession in Florin is unknown.

Japanese farmers broke through unforgiving clay hardpan to plant crops and develop irrigation. Advancements in local agriculture that led to specialization in strawberry and grape cultivation were due in part to the influx of immigrant labor from cities and the expansion of irrigation. As a result, many of Florin's farmers were able to scale up their operations.

Many grapevines flourish in the hot Florin sun on the Kishaba farm and vineyard in this undated photograph. The Kishaba farm was in "South Florin," on the western side of the railroad tracks south of Gerber Road. A grouping of other family farms included the Isa, Nakamura, Sakakihara, Nobuso, Kadokawa, and Nakaya families.

Japanese strawberry cultivation techniques achieved results that Florin's white farmers did not attain in previous years. Japanese methods of digging deep ditches to retain moisture and aligning the rows of strawberries on an east-west axis for longer sun exposure resulted in earlier harvests and a prolonged season.

Electricity was brought to Florin in 1906 and further modernized Florin's growing and shipping methods, which catapulted the township's products to the world stage. By 1908, the year this photograph was taken, Iwao Takahama and Zensaku Teranishi jointly purchased this Florin farm. The water pump transformer for an irrigation well that is being dug sits on the right, and two men are standing to the left.

Masao and Sumiko Taniguchi's farm was in an area called Taishoku, north and slightly east of Florin's business center. Taishoku was a term sometimes used to refer to the greater Florin region. Masao Taniguchi and his horse, shown in this c. 1938 photograph, no doubt spent many hours tending to difficult farm duties.

Strawberries and grapes dominated the Florin landscape and buoyed its agricultural economy between 1900 and 1942. This c. 1925 image shows rows of grapevines destined to produce raisins, wine, or simply fresh-picked table grapes to be shipped to markets around the country, including the East Coast.

The Taishoku farmhouse and outbuildings in this undated photograph appear to be in the process of being consumed by thickly growing grapevines. Some Issei farmers were able to buy their own properties before the 1913 Alien Land Act, which prohibited Japanese immigrants without citizen status from owning land or leasing it for longer than three years. Japanese immigrants were not allowed to naturalize under federal law at this time.

Masao Taniguchi and his son Roy stand outside their family home in this undated photograph. The Taniguchi family tended their own farm but also worked on the Oji hop ranch in Mayhew, north of the town center of Florin and near the American River. When forced removal occurred in 1942 due to anti-Japanese racism and Executive Order 9066, the Taniguchis were sent to the Fresno "Assembly" Center and then to the Jerome incarceration camp in Arkansas.

Roy T. Hayoshi takes a moment for this 1935 photograph showing him balancing strawberry crates as he works on Masao Taniguchi's farm. Strawberry cultivation and harvesting was grueling work that Japanese immigrants were willing to perform in order to build economic security and a stable future for themselves and their families.

With riding boots and motorcycle panniers packed, Roy Hayoshi might be ready for a trip. This c. 1923 photograph shows him sitting outside the International Harvester farm machines store.

Perhaps on a scenic ride or maybe gathered to handle business, these young Florin men travel in style. Most are unidentified, except for Sadaichi Okimura (in back, highest seated), Yuichi Mizoguchi (center, hand on face), and Masaichi Uchida (at steering wheel). Uchida and his wife, Shizu, ran a large farm off Florin Road between French Road and Gardner Avenue.

This undated portrait captures a group of farmers and possibly business owners from Florin. From left to right are (first row) Mr. Mukai, Mr. Oto, Mr. Tanigawa, Masaichi Uchida, and Mr. Enkoji; (second row) Mr. Kuroko, Mr. Mito, Mr. Kodama, Mr. Goishi, and Yuichi Mizoguchi. Masaichi Uchida and Mr. Mukai were farmers.

One Fujii farm is listed just north of Elder Creek and Power Inn Roads, and two others were in the southeast agricultural area of Florin. It is unclear which of these farms is pictured here. If this 1945 photograph was taken by Richard Fujii, it would have been after the Japanese American exclusion order lapsed and incarceration camps had released detainees, some of whom returned to Florin. Neat rows of grapevines grow in the foreground.

Professor Matsuoka gave an agricultural lecture at the Mayhew Community Center, shown in this 1940s photograph. From left to right are (first row) Mrs. Matsumoto, Kinue Iwasa, Mrs. Igarashi, Reverend Igarashi, Professor Matsuoka, two unidentified, and Mr. Sakuma; (second row) Mr. Furuike, Sadao Fred Matsumoto, Richard Fujii, Masami Iwasa, Masateru Hoshimoto, unidentified, Roy Kawamura, Yosuo Hashimoto, unidentified, Noboru Matsumoto, and Riichi Satow; (third row) Shinji Sato, unidentified, Hideo Machida, T. Hashimoto, Hisata Iwasa, and four unidentified; (fourth row) Mr. Toguchi, Mr. Ogawa, Mr. Kobata with Gladys ?, unidentified, and Mr. Matsumoto.

The Fujii farm's outbuildings are shown in this 1945 photograph. On the right is a chicken coop with a tall water tower to its left, and part of a second house is visible on the left with much of it out of frame. Some Japanese farmers were able to make arrangements with white friends and neighbors to maintain their farms through the duration of incarceration.

This photograph of Richard Fujii's farm in 1945 gives a straight-on view of the large barn with rows of grapevines just out of frame to the right. An automobile or piece of farm machinery is just out of sight inside the barn. On the left is a full side view of the second house that was built on the property.

Ground-breaking for the Florin Buddhist Church occurred on November 3, 1919, and construction was completed on March 20, 1920. A new temple was constructed in 1976 to accommodate increasing numbers of church members. The Florin Buddhist Church celebrated its 100th anniversary in 2019 with the opening of a 37-year-old copper time capsule that included a photo album and newspaper clippings. Church and community members also celebrated the Obon Festival, which recognizes that the souls of the departed are present for three days before returning to their resting place. This photograph was taken between 1919, when the church was founded, and 1925.

This undated portrait features Rev. Gyosei Nagafuji, who was minister of the Florin Buddhist Church between 1934 and 1940. The church's first minister was Rev. Kakudo Sugiyama, who served from October 1918 to January 1919. The church was not only a place of worship but also a community gathering place.

This 1942 photograph focuses on Rev. Shozen Naito's hands as he secures a padlock on the doors of the Florin Buddhist Church. After World War II, Dr. Masayoshi Ito and his wife, Shizuko Grace, donated part of their property to the Florin Buddhist Church to build a new Buddhist temple and multipurpose room. (Photograph by Dorothea Lange, courtesy of Densho.org.)

Sports and club activities were popular with Nisei, who participated in many youth organizations. This c. 1940 team photograph shows the members of the Florin Bluettes of the Florin Young Women's Buddhist Association (YWBA). Only two players in the first row have been identified: Mary Kawamura (second from left) and Natsuye Tanaka (far right).

The trophy and happy faces speak for themselves in this 1934 Young Buddhist Association (YBA) baseball team photograph. Two of the jerseys are monogrammed with a stylized letter "F." The YBA was established in 1928, the same year as the 10th-anniversary service of the Florin Buddhist Church. The YBA was reactivated in 1946 with the purpose of reawakening religious and social activities after the community persevered through World War II incarceration.

Ichiro Miyagawa and Fred Balhorn stand in front of the new Young Buddhist Association Hall in this March 12, 1939, photograph. Gakuen Hall, a former social hall and Japanese language school, was demolished in preparation for the new YBA Hall. Small international flags decorate the YBA Hall as part of the dedication celebration taking place on the day of this photograph.

The Florin Methodist Church King's Daughters Club stands with the church building in the background in this 1924 photograph. The church's first pastor was Rev. Reiichi Manabe. Rev. Kosaburo Baba, an evangelist, shepherded the congregation through the difficult years of the Great Depression during the 1930s.

This large group of Sunday school attendants is posed in front of the Florin Japanese Methodist Church in 1928. The church was built in 1915 and established a Japanese language school at a cost of 25¢ per month in 1913. The first three students were Yoshio Kiino, Ume Kawamoto, and Teichi Yasui, but by 1914, the school enrolled 35 students.

This c. 1930 photograph captures a wedding reception in the newly built Florin Japanese Community Hall, an annex of the adjacent Florin Japanese Methodist Church. The 1928 construction of the social hall was headed by Kuzo Tsukamoto. Members brought their belongings to be stored in the community hall in 1942 in preparation for their forced removal to detention camps.

Kohana Sasaki wrote, directed, did makeup, and also made costumes for performances by members of the Florin Methodist Church, such as in this 1936 portrait of the *Kasuga No Tsubone* cast. Her purpose was to teach Japanese culture through participation. Kohana Sasaki was a graduate of a prominent cultural arts teacher's college in Japan called Ochanomizu Koto Joshi Daigaku. She directed numerous Japanese dramas while her husband, Rev. Yonosuke Sasaki, ministered to families at the Florin Methodist Church. The Sasaki family—Kohana, Yonosuke, Setsuko Mildred, Shizuka Jack, Takashi Robert, Dorothy Keiko, and Junko June—spent their detention

at Tule Lake concentration camp. From left to right are (first row) Kiyoko Kiino, Emi Inouye, Julia Dakuzaku, Hatsuye Tamura, Lily Yamasaki, and Mae Yamasaki; (second row) director Sasaki Sensei, Mildred Sasaki, Jean Dakuzaku, Grace Hirabara, Miyo Nitta, Rosie Shigeno, Lily Kushi, Nami Tsukamoto, and Kazuko Kiino; (third row) Elmerine Sakakihara, Sumiko Uchida, Kinuye Tamura, Isabel Dakuzaku, Misu Kushi, and Dorothy Yamada.

The Japanese Methodist Church was across Florin Road from the Methodist church attended by Florin's white population. Segregation between Japanese and whites delineated Florin's social and economic boundaries. The children in this c. 1923 photograph attended the Florin Japanese Methodist Church. From left to right are Grace Nobuko Nitta (later Kono), Violet Chizu Ogata (Mizuki), Eileen Uchida (Fukuhara), Hazel Hanako Nishimura, Mildred Miyelo Nishimura, Doris Yuki Nitta (Taketa), and unidentified.

Young congregants of the Florin Japanese Methodist Church are pictured in 1927. These young Florinites are students from the church's kindergarten class. Little did they know that in the future, their beloved church would serve as a hostel for their own families as they sought to rebuild their lives after three years of incarceration in Japanese American concentration camps.

The 1923 graduating class at Florin Grammar School sits patiently for this group photograph. Though the new west campus (Florin West School) that was being built for white students was not completed until 1924, Florin Grammar School was already segregated, as the white students temporarily attended school at a church hall.

In 1924, a new campus of the Florin Grammar School was built for the white students. Japanese American students stayed on at the east campus. This photograph shows the 1931 graduating class. From left to right are (first row) Pauline Sakakihara, Hatsuye Nakamura, Mary Kadokawa, Doris Miyoshi, Ella Yoshinaga (valedictorian), Barbara Yamada, Misu Kushi, Katherine Takahashi, Elsie Seno, and Nami Tsukamoto; (second row) Rosie Shigeno, Frank Yuemura, Shigeso Ishii, Kaoru Shintaku, Elora Margetts (principal from 1923 to 1939), Margaret Sentani, Fred Fukushima, Henry Sakakihara, Albert Hirohata, and Hayami Kurima.

The Sierra School was built in 1912 in the northern region of the greater Florin area at Jackson Road and Hedge Avenue. Students from Perkins, Mayhew, Brighton, and Taishoku attended Sierra School. This 1925 photograph shows students of different ages with their teacher, at center in the back.

Sierra School students in the sixth, seventh, and eighth grades pose with their teacher and principal, Dorothy Love Mack, who is standing at far right in the first row. This 1932 photograph shows that the majority of the student body were Nisei. Principal Mack was a former student at Sierra School, having enrolled three years after the school was established.

This 1939 portrait of Sierra School's seventh- and eighth-grade classes was taken three years before Japanese American exclusion. Up until the 1942 forced removal, Sierra School was growing and hiring additional teachers. However, by 1944, only two teachers and 48 students remained.

Kazuo Inouye (left) and Louis Seto play in cowboy outfits in this c. 1930 photograph. Anti-Japanese rhetoric accused Japanese Americans of resisting assimilation into American culture, but this image demonstrates the opposite. Kazuo was one of three siblings; his two sisters were Yoriko and Futsuko. Their father, Isaburo Inouye, also raised one of their orphaned cousins, Oscar Asao.

Florin High School's varsity football team is in position and ready to practice a play in this 1931 photograph. Homes topped by gabled and hipped roofs sit in the distance. The current Florin High School opened in 1989 and is part of the Elk Grove Unified School District, but is not located in Florin.

This 1926 photograph shows Florin Grammar School's girls' baseball team posing with a trophy. Part of the caption states "East School," which refers to the segregated Japanese campus. The west school was for white students only. Principal J.E. Kaler stands in the back. From left to right are (first row) May Maruki, Amy Murakami, Frances Seno, and Shizue Kadokawa; (second row) Ruth Dakuzaku, Bernice Fukushima, Alice Yamada, Mary Tanihara, and Ruby Uchida.

This 1915 photograph captures one of Florin's Japanese American baseball teams. Identified are Yoshio Kino, George Yasui, Rev. Reiichi Manabe, Mr. Hayashi, Y. Tsuda, Mr. Yutaka, George Etsuzo (Kadokawa) Tsukamoto, Yosh Ouchida, Mr. Nishida, and Frank Yoshida, who attended Florin Grammar School and was the first Japanese American student to graduate from Elk Grove High School.

Florin baseball players are shown here holding their pennant around 1923. Sports teams were often organized through churches such as the Florin Buddhist Church and the Mayhew Community Baptist Church. Athletic participation was popular with Florin families, and Florin's baseball teams were consistently top performers over decades of competition.

The five trophies on display in this c. 1925 team portrait leave little doubt of Florin baseball's record of success. Players from farming families had to balance their share of work on the farm or ranch with their other pursuits. Much of life was segregated in Florin, including churches, schools, and sports.

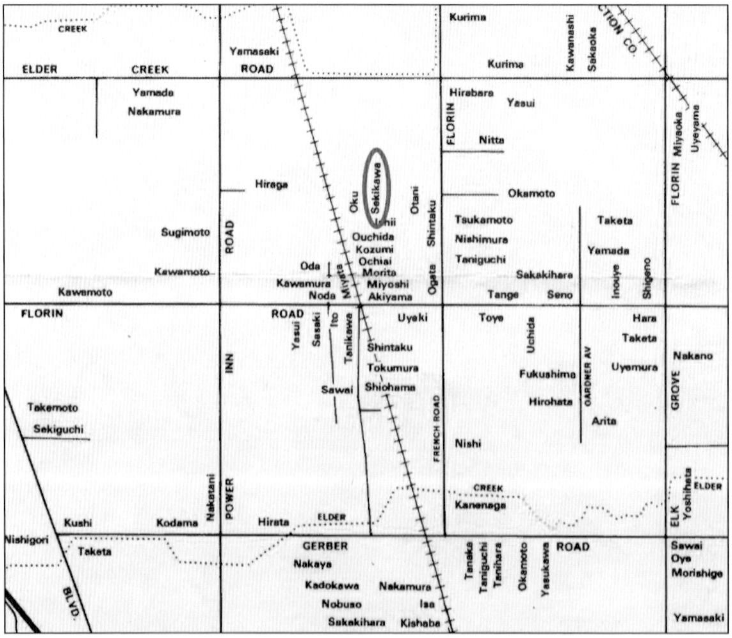

Genkichi and Fudeyo Sekikawa married in Seattle, Washington, in 1913 and purchased 22 acres of Florin farmland in the early 1920s. Their property was west of Florin Perkins Road and east of the Southern Pacific railroad tracks. Genkichi Sekikawa was a baseball fan who loved to watch his sons play. Fortunately, Florin's baseball diamond was at the entrance of the Sekikawa farm at Florin Perkins Road.

Rev. Jokai Kow stands in the center of this team portrait holding the 1934 Rural League championship trophy. Reverend Kow was assigned to the Florin Buddhist Church from August to November 1925. Florin's baseball teams were a winning force throughout the decades, with teams representing the agricultural region surrounding the town of Florin. Baseball teams were even reorganized after Japanese Americans returned from their time at detention camps during World War II.

Three

FLORIN'S FARMING FAMILIES

Mary (Dakuzaku) Tsukamoto moved to Florin with her family in 1925 from Turlock, California. Here, she toils under the hot sun picking strawberries with her mother and siblings. From left to right are mother Kame Dakuzaku, George, Mary, Jean, and Isabel. These children grew up under the harsh reality of anti-Japanese racism that worsened as Japanese farmers became more successful. Mary was 27 with a young daughter, Marielle Bliss, when Florin experienced forced removal. Wanting to transform her difficult experiences into a tool for teaching others, she became an activist for peace, civil rights, and redress after exclusion. Her legacy was commemorated by the establishment of the Mary Tsukamoto Elementary School in Elk Grove.

This 1918 Tanaka family portrait shows Sekiyo Tanaka holding her baby Wilbert (Toshio), with Tomokichi Tanaka's hand on his son George's shoulder. The Tanakas both came from Hiroshima, Japan. They grew grapes and strawberries in Florin until 1931, when they moved to Gerber Road and built a two-story home. The family was sent to the Arboga temporary detention camp near Marysville, then Jerome concentration camp in Arkansas, and finally to the Heart Mountain concentration camp in Wyoming. After their release from Heart Mountain in 1945, the Tanakas returned to their ranch on Gerber Road and resumed farming.

Sadaichi and Makiyo Okimura farmed in the area of Taishoku, just off Hedge Avenue and slightly north of Fruitridge Road. Forced removal in 1942 sent the Okimuras to the Fresno temporary detention center and then to the Jerome incarceration camp in Arkansas. Siblings Alice, Teimei, Keiso, Noboru, and Samuel all accompanied their parents, but Shigenobu enlisted in the US Army in 1942 and therefore was not detained in the camps. This family portrait was taken around 1945.

This is the portrait of a woman who immigrated to a foreign country and had the life she worked many hard years to build torn apart by racism. After the closing of detention camps, many families went their separate ways with the common goal of rebuilding their lives. By 1969, the year this photograph was taken, Fusa Ishikawa had traveled this difficult path.

Issei Fusa Ishiguro is shown with her 1900 cohort of fellow missionary school graduates. The missionary school was in Japan. She is seated in the first row, fifth from right. Fusa Ishiguro became Fusa Ishikawa in 1908 with her marriage to Saijiro. Together, they raised a family of five children. Their youngest son was named Woodrow Ishikawa.

Fusa and Saijiro Ishikawa are seated together in this 1951 postwar photograph. Saijiro Ishikawa, a native of Toyama Prefecture, Japan, immigrated to San Francisco in the early 1900s. He moved to Sacramento around 1905 and purchased farmland to grow grapes at 9010 Tokay Lane. Tokay Lane was a short road that ran perpendicular to the east set of railroad tracks owned by the Central California Traction Company.

Hisata and Kinue Iwasa, pictured in this undated portrait, married in 1915 and moved to Mayhew in 1930 to cultivate grapes and strawberries. Kinue Iwasa was a picture bride.

Hisata Iwasa passed away on February 18, 1942, leaving behind his wife and children. He immigrated from Fukuoka Prefecture, Japan, to Hawaii, Los Angeles, Fresno, and eventually the Florin area. Hisata Iwasa took part in establishing the Mayhew Sunday School, Northern California Berry Growers, the Florin Fruit Growers Association, and Florin Wine Growers Association.

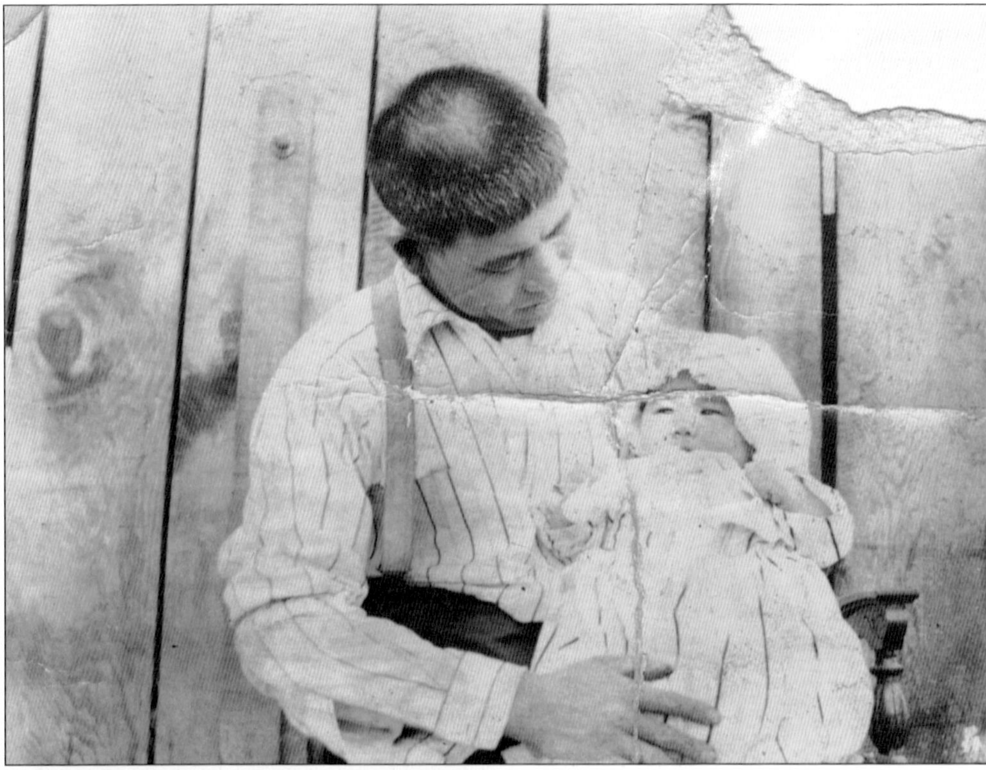

Hisata Iwasa and his wife, Kinue, had six children before he passed away in 1942. This c. 1920 photograph shows him holding his first born, a daughter named Kaoru Iwasa. It appears that Hisata's shirt and Kaoru's dress are endearingly made of the same striped material.

The Iwasa children pose for this 1926 sibling portrait. Farm life in Florin meant that all family members were part of the labor pool. School, sports, clubs, and agricultural work often made up the daily routine for many Florin children. From left to right are Kiyoka, Miyo, Kaoru, Yoshio, and Masami.

As the years went on, the Iwasa family grew, and this c. 1928 photograph shows mother Kinue Iwasa with her children. Hisata Iwasa died in February 1942, the same year Kinue Iwasa and her children were sent to the Pinedale "Assembly" Center and thereafter to Poston incarceration camp in Arizona. From left to right are Masami, Kaoru Bernice, Yoshio, Kinue, Miyo Frances, and Kiyoka.

Hide Nitta was Kazo Kadokawa's picture bride and arrived in Florin in 1909 from Japan. She had four children, but only three survived: Agnes Shizue (1911), Ted Hideo (1913), and Mary Kazumi (1915). This 1911 portrait shows their young family with baby Shizue. Kazo immigrated to the United States in 1900 at the age of 23 after working in Canada long enough to save the money needed to join his sister and brother-in-law, Ito and Kuzo Tsukamoto, in Florin. Siblings Kazo and Ito were from Yokohama, Japan.

Kazo Kadokawa joined Kuzo Tsukamoto and Shonosuke Kushi as business partners in owning 60 acres of farmland at the corner of Stockton Boulevard and Gerber Road in 1906. As the Kadokawa family grew, Kazo sold his portion and purchased 30 acres of his own in south Florin, where he and his brother in law Joichi Nitta toiled for months preparing the land for farming. Kazo's picture bride, Hide, died in 1919, a victim of the influenza pandemic, and Kazo married Misuno Kamidoi. From left to right in this 1922 family portrait are Agnes Yamada, Misuno (Kamidoi) Kadokawa, Mary Ishigaki, Bertha Makaki, Ted Hideo Kadokawa, Kazo Kadokawa, and Alice Omachi.

This 1902 portrait shows Kazo Kadokawa with his nephew Etsuzo (Kadokawa) Tsukamoto. Kazo Kadokawa did not survive to experience the forced removal of all Japanese American Florinites from their beloved farmland in 1942. Kazo and Hide's middle child, Ted Hideo, and his family were first sent to Fresno "Assembly" Center on May 29, 1942. By October 6 of the same year, they were moved to the Jerome concentration camp, and then to Rohwer, Arkansas, a year and a half later. Hideo and his family returned to Florin in August 1945.

This 1915 portrait of the Kanekichi and Hatsu (Fujikami) Tsukamoto family includes two of their first three children, baby Shizue (born 1914) and Sam (born 1912). Their first daughter, Katsuko, born in 1910, is not pictured because she was sent to Iwakuni, Japan, to care for her grandparents and receive an education. Kankekichi was born in Iwakuni in 1888 and traveled to Hawaii when he was 20 years old. Hatsu Fujikami arrived as a picture bride, and the family lived in Suisun, Courtland, and Sacramento County before settling in south Florin at the Eleven Oaks Ranch around 1928.

The Tsukamoto family had grown by the time this portrait was taken in 1929. Katsuko, who was sent to Japan when she was five years old, returned to her family in south Florin in 1929. Around 1931, Kanekichi Tsukamoto purchased 20 acres to raise strawberries, grapes, and lettuce. The Tsukamotos were forced into concentration camps at Jerome and then Rohwer in Arkansas, and returned to Florin around 1945. From left to right are (first row) Kanekichi, Yoshio, Bill, Rose, and Hatsu holding baby Jim; (second row) Shizue, Kanekichi's nephew Tadao, Isamu, Sam, Katsuko, and Teru.

Yoshio Tsukamoto poses in front of what might be a dugout in this 1939 photograph. Florin had a baseball diamond at the Sekikawa farm. The team won numerous rural league championships both before the May 1942 forced removal of Japanese Americans and after the exclusion order was lifted and players returned to Florin.

Four of Kanekichi and Hatsu Tsukamoto's sons were Florin baseball players, and all are pictured in this 1949 post-incarceration photograph. It is said that Kanekichi Tsukamoto did not abide laziness and was proud that his sons were athletes representing Florin. From left to right are (first row) Bill and Yosh; (second row) Jim and Sam. Kanekichi Tsukamoto, who valued discipline and hard work, sent his sons to pick wine grapes even after playing Friday-night football games.

This 1917 photograph shows a young Dakuzaku family with Kame holding Mary (age two) and her sister Ruth (age four) standing beside them. Taro stands behind Ruth, Nobuko Oraku is seated to the right, and Chosin Dakuzaku is seated at far right. Brothers Taro and Chosin and friends from Okinawa had a laundry business in San Francisco.

Chosei Taro and Kame (Yoshinaga) Dakuzaku were part owners of Capitol Laundry in San Francisco before eventually settling in Florin in 1925 as strawberry farmers. This 1916 photograph captures a family dinner and shows Mary and her sister, Ruth, in the foreground. Taro Dakuzaku admired Pres. Abraham Lincoln, whose portrait can be seen on the wall in the background.

Before the Dakuzaku family moved to Florin, they had a melon farm in Turlock. This August 15, 1920, photograph shows that farming was a family effort. The Dakuzakus moved to Florin for a new beginning, first leasing from a farmer named Jenkins on Gerber Road and then purchasing an adjacent farm of their own.

A new house was built for the Dakuzaku family by builder Mr. Nakamura with the help of Chosin Dakuzaku, Kokan Oshiro, and Hideo Kohagura. The Dakuzaku home was built on Gerber Road in southwest Florin. The Dakuzaku farm produced strawberries and grapes. The Dakuzakus and Tsukamotos were sent together to the Fresno temporary detention center.

This Dakuzaku family portrait was taken around 1929, after the family moved to Florin from Turlock. By this time, the family had grown. From left to right are (first row) Jean Yoshiko, Julia Toshiko, Kame (Yoshinaga), George Tomomitsu, and Chosei Taro; (second row) Isabel Sumiko, Mary Tsuruko, and Ruth Haruko.

Mary Tsukamoto's parents, Chosei Taro and Kame Dakuzaku, moved from Chicago, Illinois, to Kalamazoo, Michigan, to join their daughter and her family as the Tsukamotos began a life of new freedom after their detention at the Jerome concentration camp in Arkansas. Mary's sister Julia and brother George also lived with them in Kalamazoo. This 1943 photograph shows Chosei and Kame Dakuzaku in Chicago.

Mary and Al Tsukamoto pose in front of a pond in Los Angeles in 1938. Mary (Dakuzaku) Tsukamoto's parents had a strawberry farm in Florin. She became a teacher, activist, and speaker and was the impetus for establishing the Japanese American Archival Collection at California State University, Sacramento.

Mary Tsuruko Dakuzaku and Alfred Iwao Tsukamoto married in 1936 and had Marielle Bliss Tsukamoto in 1937. This October 1944 portrait of Mary and Marielle Tsukamoto was taken just before they departed the concentration camp at Jerome to join Alfred Tsukamoto in Kalamazoo in November. The US Army anticipated that Executive Order 9066 would lapse and allowed detainees to search for and take jobs before the closure of the concentration camps was officially announced. Mary's parents, Chosei Taro Dakuzaku and Kame Yoshinaga, married in 1904, the same year Chosei Dakuzaku immigrated to the United States. Kame Dakuzaku, however, did not join her husband until 1917. Mary Tsuruko's siblings were Masako (who remained in Japan), Ruth Haruko, Isabel Sumiko, Jean Yoshiko, Julia Toshiko, and George Tomomistu.

The list of duties required to keep a farm up and running was long and varied, and this undated photograph shows Issei Kuzo Tsukamoto and family members standing on a flatbed as they spray fruit trees. It was common among Florin agricultural families for all family members to contribute to keeping the farm running.

Ito Tsukamoto stands while husband Kuzo Tsukamoto kneels over an abundant strawberry crop. The Tsukamotos were married in 1895 in Hiroshima and had settled in the Florin area on Gerber Road by 1902. Their son Alfred married Mary Dakuzaku. Florin's summer heat and the strenuous hours of bending over the short crops made strawberry farming rewarding but not without challenges.

Heisaburo Okamoto (left) and Fusano (Noso) Okamoto were both from Hiroshima, Japan. Heisaburo Okamoto labored at a Hawaiian sugar plantation before arriving in North America in 1902. He worked on the transcontinental railroad through the Feather River Canyon until the hazards of the job became too great and he made his way to Florin. Fusano Noso arrived in Florin as a picture bride. The 1920 family portrait below shows, from left to right (first row) M. Tange, Sam Isamu, Joe Kazuma, Bill Takeshi, and Grace Michika; (second row) S. Nakashima, Fusano Okamoto, and Heisaburo Okamoto. In 1920, the family acquired 40 acres off Florin Perkins Road where they built their home and a barn and grew grapes and strawberries. The family was productive enough to purchase more land on Gerber Road in 1927, but it was not as fruitful. The Okamotos were incarcerated first at the Fresno "Assembly" Center and then at Jerome and Rohwer camps in Arkansas.

Fusano (Noso) Okamoto and her son Sam are shown standing in front of the birthplace of the Okamoto children in 1914. Born here were Isamu (Sam) in 1913, Kazuma (Joe) in 1914, Takeshi (Bill) in 1915, and Michika (Grace) in 1918. The Okamotos share-cropped on the John E. Thomas ranch on Gerber Road, where husband and wife worked the land together with an eye toward having a place of their own.

Florinite Bob Fletcher (1911–2013) managed the Okamoto, Nitta, and Tsukamoto (Alfred and Mary) farms during the years of Japanese American exclusion, 1942–1945. His agriculture degree from what would become the University of California, Davis, and ranch management and agriculture inspection experience equipped him to quickly learn grape farming. Fletcher's new wife, Teresa Cassieri, helped to manage the 90 acres. Together, the Fletchers made mortgage and tax payments and saved half of the profits for the families' return even though the agreement was for him to keep all profits. (Courtesy of Marielle Tsukamoto.)

Brothers Koyei (Tom, left) and Kokan Oshiro pose together in this 1929 photograph taken in San Francisco to mark Tom's high school graduation. The brothers' Issei parents, father Kojo Oshiro and mother Komato (Kaneshiro) Oshiro, emigrated from Okinawa, Japan. Kojo Oshiro became wealthy through melon farming but lost it all when he tried the same with hog farming, causing Komato Oshiro to return to Okinawa and the brothers to be put under the guardianship of a family friend. Kojo Oshiro died in the 1918 influenza pandemic.

The Takehara family gathered in 1935 for this group portrait. From left to right are (first row) Tom, father Kikumatsu, Bessie, mother Tami, and George; (second row) Paul, Bertha, Herb, Kikue, and Jim. Like many Japanese American families, World War II and incarceration sent family members to different parts of the country.

Pictured here is a gathering of friends and family at the Takehara family home in July 1930. The group is standing to the side of the front entrance stairs. Kikumatsu and Tami Takehara owned a 45-acre farm north of Florin near Jackson and Bradshaw where they grew strawberries and grapes.

This c. 1935 photograph of the Takehara family's house and farm provides another view of their property. The baluster from the previous photograph is fully visible, as are outbuildings and the automobile in the driveway. The Takehara siblings included Masashi Herbert, Chiyoko Bertha, James Torao, Doris Kikuye, Paul, Tom, George, and Bessie Miyoko.

Kikumatsu Takehara stands in front of his new automobile in 1927. The image provides a close-up of the car and details of the house in the previous photograph such as the exposed rafter tails and six-over-six double-hung windows.

Chiyoko Takehara picks strawberries on a sunny June day in this 1932 photograph taken on the family property. The difficult stoop labor required for strawberry cultivation and harvesting was done by all able family members, including young children. Issei farmers often could not afford to hire many workers, and using free family labor was one way to overcome this obstacle.

The smiling faces of the Takehara family reflect their hard-earned success and hope for their children's future in this c. 1935 photograph. This image was captured before Executive Order 9066 was signed, forcibly removing all of Florin's Japanese American families from the lives they had worked tirelessly to build.

Ranch and farm labor required the work of many hands, and the Takehara farm was no different. This c. 1941 photograph shows friends taking a break together. Crates labeled "Takehara" are stacked on the truck bed. From left to right are Silver, Gladys, Mrs. Huber, Orrie, Toby, and brothers Russ and Jim Fairbairn. The Fairbairn farm was near the Takehara property.

Kikumatsu and Tami Takehara, along with other community members, send their son Paul Takehara off to begin his service with the US Army. This photograph, taken on March 7, 1941, shows concerned expressions on the faces of the Takeharas, who are standing together at center wearing dark jackets.

Masao and Ichi Taketa were fruit farmers in Florin until Masao became an insurance agent and the family moved to Sacramento. This 1918 photograph was taken shortly before Ichi and her children, (from left to right) Tom, Henry, and Akiko May, visited Japan. Henry, born on January 5, 1912, was an attorney for 50 years and maintained his law license during Japanese exclusion.

This 1918 Taketa family portrait captures their visit to Hiroshima, Japan, where Ichi Taketa visited her father after having lived in the United States for 16 years. It was common for family members, even husbands and wives, to live in separate countries for many years. From left to right are May, Henry, Ichi, and Tom Taketa.

The Taketa family was sent to the Walerga temporary detention center (Walerga "Assembly" Center, also called Sacramento "Assembly" Center) in Sacramento and then to the Tule Lake incarceration camp in Northern California near the Oregon border. Tule Lake was designated a national historic landmark in 2006. Parents Masao (left) and Ichi (right) are seated in the front row, with Tom, May, and Henry (left to right) standing. Tom Taketa left for the University of California, Berkeley, not long after this 1930 photograph was taken.

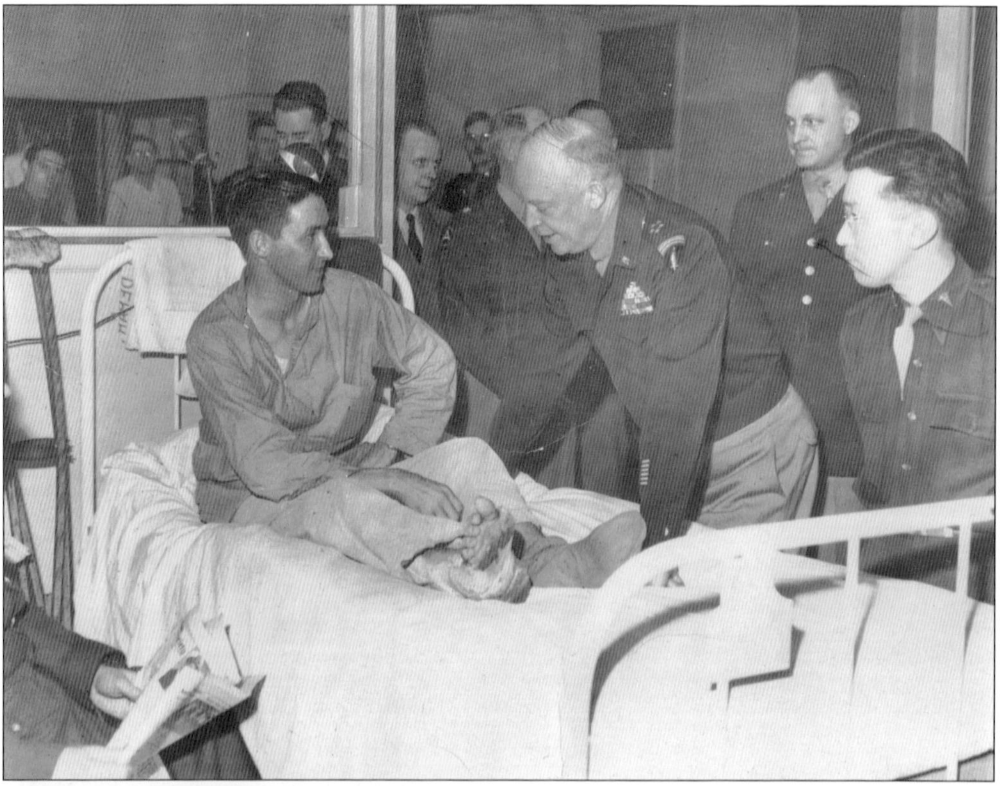

Dr. Tom Taketa is standing next to Gen. Dwight D. Eisenhower as he talks with an injured soldier. This 1946 photograph documents Eisenhower touring hospitals and exhibiting one of his recognized strengths as a leader, public relations. Note the Army Medical Corps insignia on Dr. Taketa's collar.

Masaichi and Shizu Uchida pose with their first child, daughter Mary Uchida, in this 1911 family portrait. In addition to Mary, the Uchida siblings would eventually include Elmer, George, Leo, David, Daniel, Ruth, and Ruby. Through marriage, the Uchida family extended to the Nakanos of West Sacramento and the Kiinos of Florin.

Masaichi Uchida sold his farm for $4,000 before forced removal to the Manzanar concentration camp. Manzanar, a national historic site since 1992, incarcerated up to 10,000 Japanese Americans. It is in the Owens Valley, an area indigenous to Shoshone and Paiute, and sits at elevations between 3,800 and 4,200 feet above sea level. Many of California's Japanese Americans were not used to the cold and wet winters in the higher elevations.

Masaichi and Shizu Uchida's farm was on the south side of Florin Road between French Road and Gardner Avenue along with other family farms such as Fukushima, Hirohata, Nishi, and Toye. This area was between two sets of railroad tracks, one used by the Southern Pacific and the other by the Central California Traction Company. Friends, family, and neighbors are gathered in this 1917 photograph.

This 1935 portrait of Ruth Uchida shows her at the Weimar Sanatorium in Placer County, California, a hospital where tuberculosis patients who could not afford private medical care received treatment. Depending on the severity of the case, patients might have stayed for many years.

Masaichi Uchida seems quite content with his catch of the day in this undated photograph. Perhaps he spent time at the American River on the day this photograph was taken. The river, to the north of Florin, provided excellent habitat for native chinook salmon and steelhead trout.

The context of this photograph showing Choji Kawada riding a bicycle in Elk Grove around 1900 is unknown, but it is fun to study. Onlookers have horses and a cart, and there is one other bicycle in the picture. Interesting barns and other structures with gabled and hipped roofs can be seen in the background.

Choji and Mitsuye Kawada were early farmers in the Florin area. This c. 1905 portrait captures the couple, who farmed 40 acres of beans but were discouraged by flooding and moved away, according to Charles Kawada. Their farm was north of Florin proper, near Folsom Boulevard and east of Sixty-Fifth Street, southwest of the railroad tracks.

Mitsuye Kawada holds a bucketful of eggs in this c. 1908 photograph. Both Mitsuye Kawada and her son Nagamitsu are turned toward the group of chickens inside the enclosure. The buildings in the background are most likely hop dryers, as hops were grown in this area.

Hisaichi Kawanishi, born in 1894, and Fusa Kawanishi, born in 1898, were Florin fruit farmers. The Kawanishi farm was on Elder Creek Road between the Kurima and Sakaoka farms and was not too far from the California Traction Company tracks. This photograph shows Hisaichi Kawanishi around 1948.

This 1952 portrait of Fusa Kawanishi shows her after the ordeal of forced removal. The Kawanishis were sent to the Fresno temporary detention facility and then to the Jerome concentration camp. The Kawanishis included Hasaichi, Fusa, Amy, Betty, Helen, James, James A., Kay, Peggy, Ruby, and Terry.

The Yamada family posed for this 1914 group portrait. Parents Kennosuke and Mikiyo Yamada are the only identified members. During the 1942 forced removal of Japanese Americans, each person was assigned an identification number, with families sharing the same number but with a letter to designate individuals. For example, the Yamadas were assigned 8699: Kennosuke (8699D), Mikiyo (8699E), Henry (8699A), and Michiye (8699B). They were sent to the Walerga "Assembly" Center and then to Tule Lake incarceration camp.

By 1900, Kumakichi (inset) and Yoshi Takeoka owned their ranch at Elder Creek Road near Hedge Avenue. The Takeokas eventually owned three ranches where they grew grapes and strawberries. Their son George returned to Japan with his retired parents in 1939 but came back in 1941 shortly before the bombing of Pearl Harbor and was incarcerated at the Fresno camp and then the Tule Lake incarceration camp.

Four

A Community in the Crosshairs

Harsh conditions at the Tule Lake incarceration camp set the backdrop of this 1943 photograph of Choji and Mistuye Kawada. The Kawadas were not sent to a temporary detention facility, known as "assembly centers," but were sent directly to Tule Lake. Their address at Tule Lake was 1402-B. Choji Kawada can be seen riding a bike through a field of tilled dirt on page 80.

C. E. Order 92

WESTERN DEFENSE COMMAND AND FOURTH ARMY
WARTIME CIVIL CONTROL ADMINISTRATION
Presidio of San Francisco, California

INSTRUCTIONS
TO ALL PERSONS OF
JAPANESE
ANCESTRY

LIVING IN THE FOLLOWING AREA:

All that portion of the Counties of Sacramento and Amador, State of California, within the boundary beginning at a point at which California State Highway No. 16 intersects California State Highway No. 49, approximately two miles south of Plymouth; thence southerly along said Highway No. 49 to the Amador-Calaveras County Line; thence westerly along the Amador-Calaveras County Line to the Amador-San Joaquin County Line; thence northerly along the Amador-San Joaquin County Line to the Sacramento-San Joaquin County Line; thence westerly along the Sacramento-San Joaquin County Line to the easterly line of the right of way of the main line of the Southern Pacific Railroad from Lodi to Sacramento; thence northerly along said easterly line to its crossing with California State Highway No. 16; thence easterly along said Highway No. 16 to point of beginning.

Pursuant to the provisions of Civilian Exclusion Order No. 92, this Headquarters, dated May 23, 1942, all persons of Japanese ancestry, both alien and non-alien, will be evacuated from the above area by 12 o'clock noon, P.W.T., Saturday, May 30, 1942.

No Japanese person will be permitted to move into, or out of, the above area after 12 o'clock noon, P.W.T., Saturday, May 23, 1942, without obtaining special permission from the representative of the Commanding General, Northern California Sector, at the Civil Control Station located at:

Masonic Hall,
Elk Grove, California.

Such permits will only be granted for the purpose of uniting members of a family, or in cases of grave emergency.

The Civil Control Station is equipped to assist the Japanese population affected by this evacuation in the following ways:

1. Give advice and instructions on the evacuation.

2. Provide services with respect to the management, leasing, sale, storage or other disposition of most kinds of property, such as real

Civilian Exclusion Order 92 commanded the forced removal of all Japanese noncitizens and Japanese Americans in the Florin area by noon on May 30, 1942. The order also dictated restrictions on travel. Special permission could be sought from the Civil Control Station inside the Elk Grove Masonic Lodge, but only for the purpose of "uniting members of a family, or in cases of grave emergency."

Photographer Dorothea Lange captured the preoccupied expression of this Florinite in 1942. The unidentified man, who arrived in the United States when he was a boy, was a father of seven children who worked in the Los Angeles wholesale grocery industry before moving to Florin. (Photograph by Dorothea Lange, courtesy of Densho.org.)

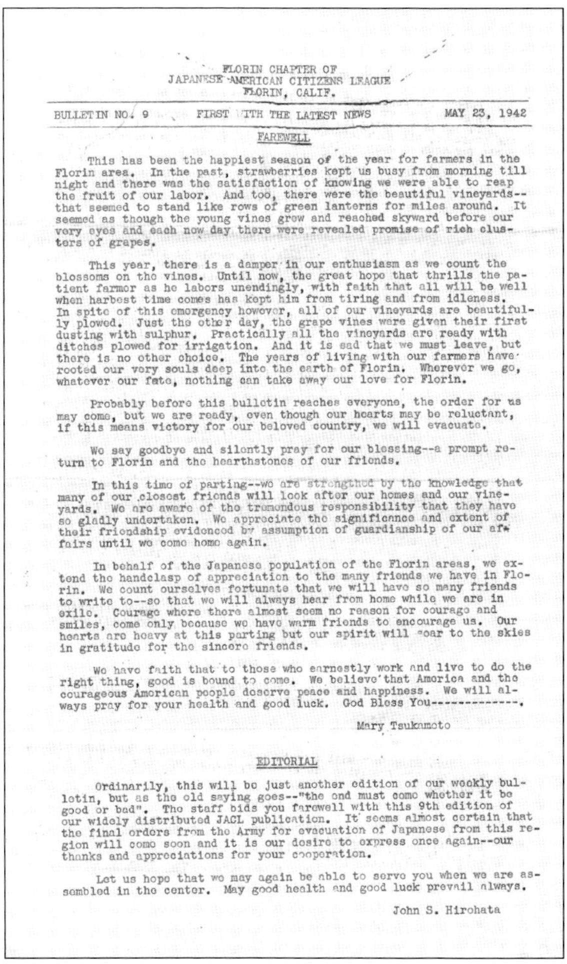

FLORIN CHAPTER OF
JAPANESE AMERICAN CITIZENS LEAGUE
FLORIN, CALIF.

BULLETIN NO. 9 FIRST WITH THE LATEST NEWS MAY 23, 1942

FAREWELL

This has been the happiest season of the year for farmers in the Florin area. In the past, strawberries kept us busy from morning till night and there was the satisfaction of knowing we were able to reap the fruit of our labor. And too, there were the beautiful vineyards--that seemed to stand like rows of green lanterns for miles around. It seemed as though the young vines grew and reached skyward before our very eyes and each new day there were revealed promise of rich clusters of grapes.

This year, there is a damper in our enthusiasm as we count the blossoms on the vines. Until now, the great hope that thrills the patient farmer as he labors unendingly, with faith that all will be well when harbest time comes has kept him from tiring and from idleness. In spite of this emergency however, all of our vineyards are beautifully plowed. Just the other day, the grape vines were given their first dusting with sulphur. Practically all the vineyards are ready with ditches plowed for irrigation. And it is sad that we must leave, but there is no other choice. The years of living with our farmers have rooted our very souls deep into the earth of Florin. Wherever we go, whatever our fate, nothing can take away our love for Florin.

Probably before this bulletin reaches everyone, the order for us may come, but we are ready, even though our hearts may be reluctant, if this means victory for our beloved country, we will evacuate.

We say goodbye and silently pray for our blessing--a prompt return to Florin and the hearthstones of our friends.

In this time of parting--we are strengthed by the knowledge that many of our closest friends will look after our homes and our vineyards. We are aware of the tremendous responsibility that they have so gladly undertaken. We appreciate the significance and extent of their friendship evidenced by assumption of guardianship of our affairs until we come home again.

In behalf of the Japanese population of the Florin areas, we extend the handclasp of appreciation to the many friends we have in Florin. We count ourselves fortunate that we will have so many friends to write to--so that we will always hear from home while we are in exile. Courage where there almost seem no reason for courage and smiles, come only because we have warm friends to encourage us. Our hearts are heavy at this parting but our spirit will soar to the skies in gratitude for the sincere friends.

We have faith that to those who earnestly work and live to do the right thing, good is bound to come. We believe that America and the courageous American people deserve peace and happiness. We will always pray for your health and good luck. God Bless You------------.

Mary Tsukamoto

EDITORIAL

Ordinarily, this will be just another edition of our weekly bulletin, but as the old saying goes--"the end must come whether it be good or bad". The staff bids you farewell with this 9th edition of our widely distributed JACL publication. It seems almost certain that the final orders from the Army for evacuation of Japanese from this region will come soon and it is our desire to express once again--our thanks and appreciations for your cooperation.

Let us hope that we may again be able to serve you when we are assembled in the center. May good health and good luck prevail always.

John S. Hirohata

This May 23, 1942, Florin Japanese American Citizens League (JACL) farewell newsletter discusses final logistics and expresses sadness at being forced to leave Florin. Despite knowing that departure was coming, farmers prepared their land as they normally would have for that part of the season. The end of the second paragraph reads, "The years of living with our farmers have rooted our very souls deep into the earth of Florin."

Japanese Americans in the Florin area were ordered to register their names and the names of family members with the Wartime Civilian Control Authority (WCCA) in preparation for their forced removal into Japanese American concentration camps. The Italianate building in this 1942 photograph was the Elk Grove Masonic Lodge, where registration took place.

This May 1942 photograph offers an opposing view of the registration taking place in the previous photograph. The people gathered here came from Florin and its neighboring communities of Mayhew, Walsh Station, Taishoku, Brighton, Perkins, Elder Creek, Jackson, California Vineyard, and Elk Grove. In 1988, Executive Order 9066 was officially deemed by the US government an act of racial discrimination against Japanese Americans.

It is difficult to imagine the stress and sadness Florinites experienced on May 29, 1942. The Elk Grove train station sent off families from all of Florin and the surrounding area with only the belongings they could carry. Homes, farms, and the majority of belongings were left behind or sold for pennies on the dollar, and those leaving their familiar communities had no idea what the future held.

Though this 1942 photograph was taken in Washington State, Florin families also were forced to leave their pets behind or even euthanize them, because pets were initially not allowed at the concentration camps. Sadly, the same fate awaited the many dogs and cats who were left behind at the camps when detainees were finally released to build new lives.

"Evacuation" instructions to Japanese Americans were to bring only what each person could carry. Imagine the excruciating choices that families faced in being forced to leave everything familiar. In addition, life carried on despite the exigencies of forced removal. For example, Florinite Mrs. Okimoto went into labor, and Sonny Ouchida was diagnosed with chicken pox. The Ouchida family quarantined in the train by staying in the women's bathroom.

Confusion and anxiety are palpable looking at the tight groupings of evacuees at the Elk Grove train station in this 1942 photograph. People dressed in their Sunday best, and many even wore coats despite the fact that it was May in the Sacramento valley. Some articles such as cribs, musical instruments, and athletic equipment were allowed to be shipped after detainees arrived at their detention camps.

In her memoir, Mary Tsukamoto describes departure day as if "I were in a movie theater watching an exodus of a people. But these people were us—families of Japanese ancestry—and we were crowded into the oddest collection of old vehicles I had ever seen. There were huge pick-ups, ancient passenger cars, and trucks loaded to capacity with personal belongings."

We the People: A Story of Internment in America, recalls May 29, 1942, as a day when so many people were stunned by the predicament forced upon them due to wartime hysteria and racism. This photograph from that day captures a moment of the fracturing of Florin's community when friends and family moved toward an unknown future.

Anxiety, powerlessness, and anger pervaded departure day for Japanese Americans in the Florin area. Families had no idea what conditions to expect in the concentration camps and feared they would be separated from family members. Nisei parents tried to maintain a sense of calm and order for the sake of their Issei parents and Sansei (third generation) children. This 1942 photograph shows people carrying luggage as they walk next to a train at the Elk Grove station.

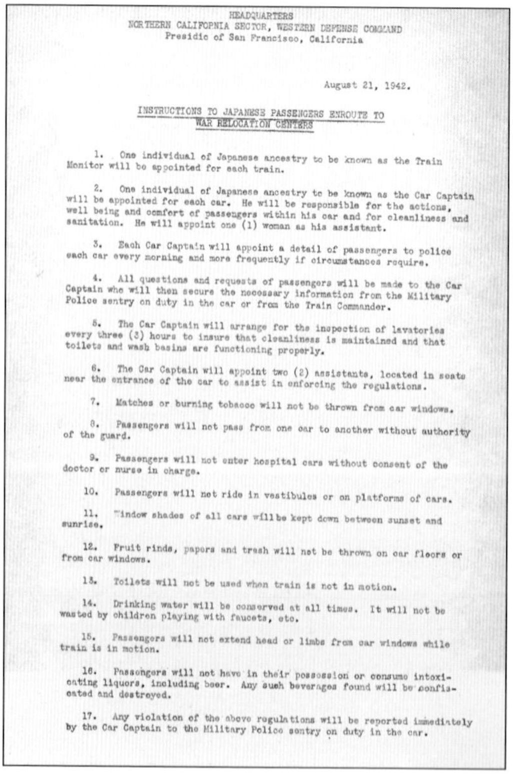

HEADQUARTERS
NORTHERN CALIFORNIA SECTOR, WESTERN DEFENSE COMMAND
Presidio of San Francisco, California

August 21, 1942.

INSTRUCTIONS TO JAPANESE PASSENGERS ENROUTE TO WAR RELOCATION CENTERS

1. One individual of Japanese ancestry to be known as the Train Monitor will be appointed for each train.

2. One individual of Japanese ancestry to be known as the Car Captain will be appointed for each car. He will be responsible for the actions, well being and comfort of passengers within his car and for cleanliness and sanitation. He will appoint one (1) woman as his assistant.

3. Each Car Captain will appoint a detail of passengers to police each car every morning and more frequently if circumstances require.

4. All questions and requests of passengers will be made to the Car Captain who will then secure the necessary information from the Military Police sentry on duty in the car or from the Train Commander.

5. The Car Captain will arrange for the inspection of lavatories every three (3) hours to insure that cleanliness is maintained and that toilets and wash basins are functioning properly.

6. The Car Captain will appoint two (2) assistants, located in seats near the entrance of the car to assist in enforcing the regulations.

7. Matches or burning tobacco will not be thrown from car windows.

8. Passengers will not pass from one car to another without authority of the guard.

9. Passengers will not enter hospital cars without consent of the doctor or nurse in charge.

10. Passengers will not ride in vestibules or on platforms of cars.

11. Window shades of all cars will be kept down between sunset and sunrise.

12. Fruit rinds, papers and trash will not be thrown on car floors or from car windows.

13. Toilets will not be used when train is not in motion.

14. Drinking water will be conserved at all times. It will not be wasted by children playing with faucets, etc.

15. Passengers will not extend head or limbs from car windows while train is in motion.

16. Passengers will not have in their possession or consume intoxicating liquors, including beer. Any such beverages found will be confiscated and destroyed.

17. Any violation of the above regulations will be reported immediately by the Car Captain to the Military Police sentry on duty in the car.

This August 1942 document is titled "Instructions to Japanese Passengers Enroute to War Relocation Centers." It lists directives in preparation for the train ride from the short-term "assembly" centers to the long-term incarceration camps. A car captain was to be selected among the detainees to serve as an intermediary between the passengers and military police. Rule number 11 states that window shades must be kept down between sunset and sunrise.

Located about 10 miles northeast of Sacramento, the Walerga temporary detention center was open for 52 days during the summer of 1942. Many Walerga detainees were sent to Tule Lake incarceration camp in Modoc County. The young woman in this 1942 photograph wrote on the back, "Our neighbor visited here and took my picture, what a background, Pam."

This page, an excerpt from an illustrated booklet created in 1945 titled *Evacuation*, was written from a young person's perspective. The illustrations recall the US Army's notification posters attached to telephone poles and the awareness of impending changes to daily life. Incarceration camp barracks lacked adequate protection from the elements. The booklet was dedicated to Margaret Gunderson, a teacher at Tule Lake High School. The creator is unknown.

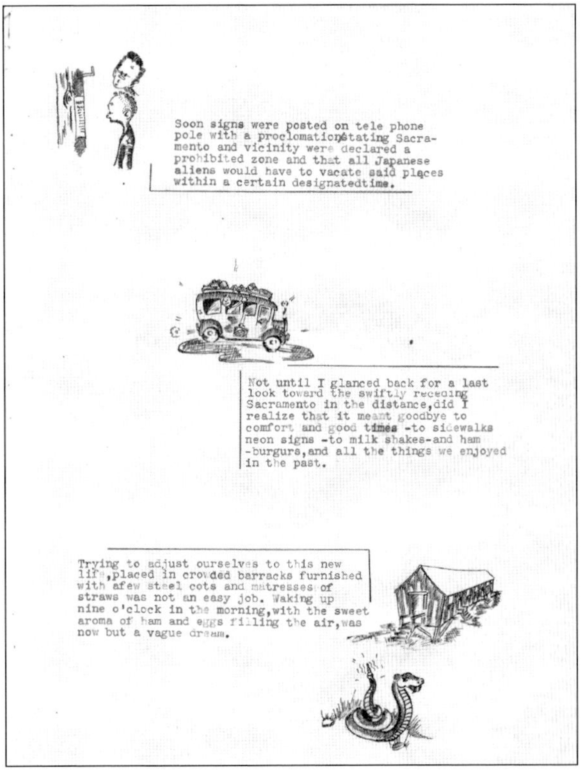

Soon signs were posted on tele phone pole with a proclomationstating Sacramento and vicinity were declared a prohibited zone and that all Japanese aliens would have to vacate said places within a certain designatedtime.

Not until I glanced back for a last look toward the swiftly receding Sacramento in the distance,did I realize that it meant goodbye to comfort and good times -to sidewalks neon signs -to milk shakes-and ham -burgurs,and all the things we enjoyed in the past.

Trying to adjust ourselves to this new life,placed in crowded barracks furnished with afew steel cots and matresses of straws was not an easy job. Waking up nine o'clock in the morning,with the sweet aroma of ham and eggs filling the air,was now but a vague dream.

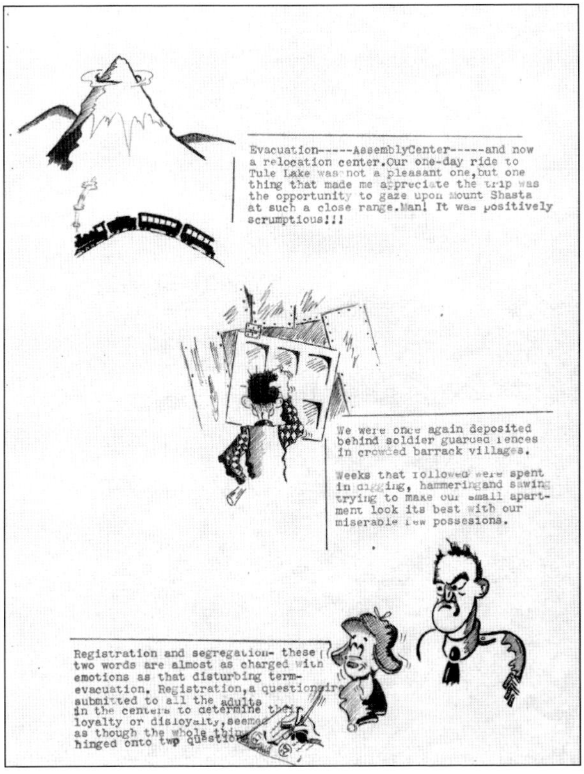

Evacuation-----AssemblyCenter-----and now a relocation center.Our one-day ride to Tule Lake was not a pleasant one,but one thing that made me appreciate the trip was the opportunity to gaze upon Mount Shasta at such a close range.Man! It was positively scrumptious!!!

We were once again deposited behind soldier guarded fences in crowded barrack villages.

Weeks that followed were spent in digging, hammeringand sawing trying to make our small apartment look its best with our miserable few possesions.

Registration and segregation- these two words are almost as charged with emotions as that disturbing term- evacuation. Registration,a questio[illegible] submitted to all the adults in the centers to determine the[illegible] loyalty or disloyalty,seeme[illegible] as though the whole thi[illegible] hinged onto twp questio[illegible]

This page recounts a first encounter with Mount Shasta during the rough train ride to the Tule Lake incarceration camp. The bottom caption refers to questions 27 and 28 of what became known as the "loyalty questionnaire." One of these questions asked if Nisei would renounce allegiance to Japan and swear allegiance to the United States. The questions were deeply resented by Nisei for the future implications of their answers.

Relationships were both strengthened and fractured by the challenges of daily life at Japanese American concentration camps. This June 1944 group photograph of Jerome residents who lived at blocks 9 and 12 captures faces of resilience. Those pictured here were either destined for another camp or preparing to relocate in free society. A number of Florin residents are in this photograph.

Many Florin families were sent to the camp in Jerome, Arkansas, after spending time at the Fresno "Assembly" Center. This c. 1943 map indicates that the area was separated into blocks. Amenities such as a gymnasium, shoe shops, judo mat, and softball and baseball fields were allowed. Detention camp activities were organized and run by the detainees.

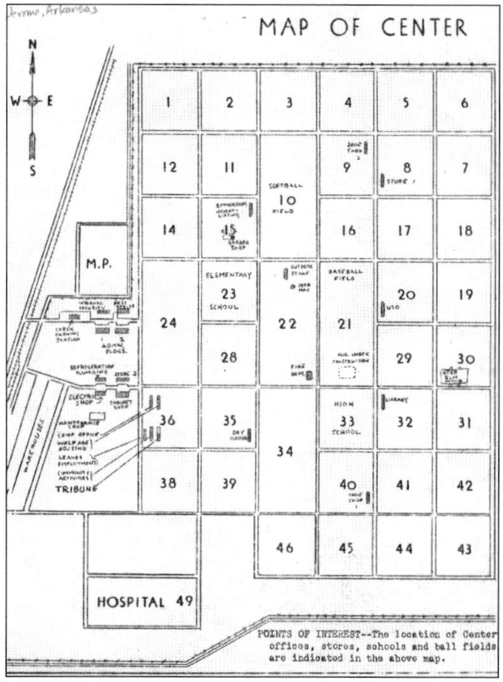

Alfred Tsukamoto is shown in 1944 visiting his family, who were still incarcerated in the Jerome "relocation" center, block 9. The Tsukamoto and Dakuzaku families moved to Kalamazoo before some returned to Florin in 1945. From left to right are (first row) Marielle Tsukamoto, Shirley Ogata, and Margaret Toshi Ogata; (second row) Alvin Ogata, Issei matriarch Ito Tsukamoto, Issei patriarch Kuzo Tsukamoto, Alfred Tsukamoto, and Arlene Ogata; (third row) Margaret Ogata, Charles Ogata, Mary Tsukamoto, and Beverly Ogata.

Taken in 1943, this photograph shows the Kuzo and Ito Tsukamoto family together in front of a row of Jerome incarceration camp barracks that appear to have been modified to create more of a feel of home. Three generations of women are captured in the image: Issei Ito Tsukamoto (front center, 65), Nisei Edith (Tsukamoto) Ouchida (back row, third from right, 35), Nisei Margaret (Tsukamoto) Ogata (back row, second from right, 37), and Sansei Lucille Ouchida (far right, 11).

Ito (Kadokawa) Tsukamoto and Kuzo Tsukamoto are pictured with their granddaughter Misa Shirley Ogata. Tarpaper barracks in the background and the dry, bare landscape set the tone of the incarceration experience in this 1944 photograph at the Jerome camp. Kuzo Tsukamoto worked in Vancouver and throughout the Pacific Northwest on railroads, in mines, and on farms before making his way to Florin in 1892.

Saijiro and Fusa Ishikawa's 30-acre Florin farm produced tokay grapes before they were sent first to Tule Lake and then to the Jerome concentration camp. From left to right in this 1945 photograph are Mary, Jin, Saijiro, Woodrow, and Fusa. Woodrow, who is in uniform, was drafted into the Army infantry in 1945 but did not serve in the 442nd Regimental Combat Team.

Matriarch Tami Takehara stands in front of barracks at the Poston, Arizona, incarceration camp in this c. 1943 photograph. The family was first sent to Pinedale temporary detention center in California before their longer-term incarceration in Arizona. Notice the tarpaper cladding of the structure behind her, which was a far cry from the spacious Takehara home.

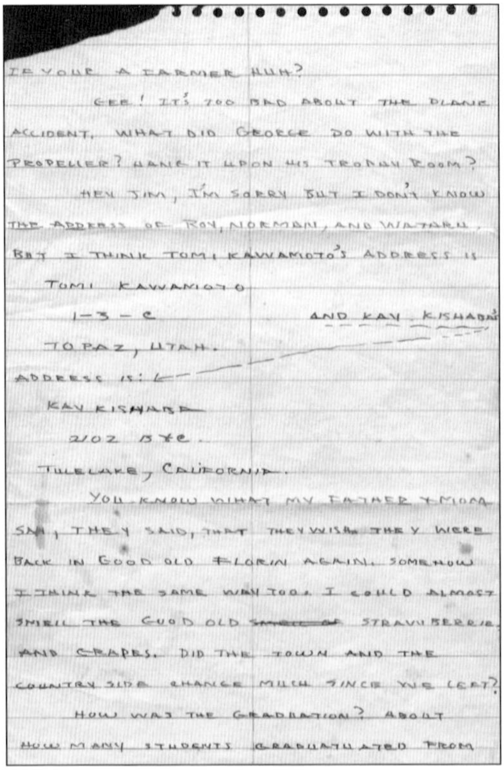

IF YOUR A FARMER HUH?
GEE! IT'S TOO BAD ABOUT THE PLANE ACCIDENT. WHAT DID GEORGE DO WITH THE PROPELLER? HANG IT UPON HIS TROPHY ROOM?
HEY JIM, I'M SORRY BUT I DON'T KNOW THE ADDRESS OF ROY, NORMAN, AND WATARU. BUT I THINK TOMI KAWAMOTO'S ADDRESS IS
TOMI KAWAMOTO
1-3-C
TOPAZ, UTAH.
AND KAY KISHABA'S ADDRESS IS:
KAY KISHABA
2102 B & C.
TULELAKE, CALIFORNIA.
YOU KNOW WHAT MY FATHER & MOM SAY, THEY SAID, THAT THEY WISH THEY WERE BACK IN GOOD OLD FLORIN AGAIN. SOMEHOW I THINK THE SAME WAY TOO. I COULD ALMOST SMELL THE GOOD OLD ~~SMELL OF~~ STRAWBERRIES AND GRAPES. DID THE TOWN AND THE COUNTRY SIDE CHANGE MUCH SINCE WE LEFT?
HOW WAS THE GRADUATION? ABOUT HOW MANY STUDENTS GRADUATUATED FROM

This June 13, 1944, letter is from Leo Uchida to James Waegell, possibly the son of Margaret and Henry Waegell who looked after the Umeda farm. Uchida wrote from the Manzanar incarceration camp, located in the Owens Valley in Central California. In the letter, Uchida expresses how he and his parents miss "good old Florin."

This photograph of former Florin resident Yank Sawamura was taken at Manzanar incarceration camp between 1942 and 1945 and shows the roughly built camp buildings. Camp conditions were primitive, vulnerable to the weather, and did not allow for much privacy. (Photograph by Dorothea Lange, courtesy of Densho.org.)

A group of Florin children are sitting in front of barracks at the Jerome "relocation" center. The sign at top left, "11-11-A," indicates the location within the camp where this 1944 photograph was taken. This would be the address used for letters to and from the family living here.

Children at Tule Lake incarceration camp pose with two crossed baseball bats in this c. 1943 photograph. Making the best of the situation, most of these young students are smiling despite the conditions. Harsh climates, barbed wire, and spartan accommodations were the defining conditions of Japanese American detention camps.

Anticipating his family's forced removal, Masaichi Uchida sold his Florin farm for $4,000 before leaving for incarceration at Manzanar concentration camp. The Uchidas joined other families who lived south of Florin Road, such as the Senos, Sakakiharas, and Matsumotos. Families from Mayhew and Walsh Station were sent to Poston concentration camp on the Colorado River Indian Reservation in Arizona. Those who lived west of the railroad tracks were sent to Tule Lake. This group photograph shows the Uchida family at Manzanar in 1944. From left to right are (first

row) Walter Nakano, Fred Nakano, Grace Nakano Seto, Ruby Uchida Nakano, Eleanor Nakano (in front), Shizu Uchida holding Carolyn Nakano Matsumura, Masaichi Uchida, Mary Uchida Kiino, Evelyn Kiino Cassaro (in front), Setsuko Nishi Uchida, and Elmer Uchida; (second row) Daniel Uchida, George Uchida, Leo Uchida, May Uchida Tominaga, Sumiye Uchida Takeno, and Eileen Uchida Fukuhara.

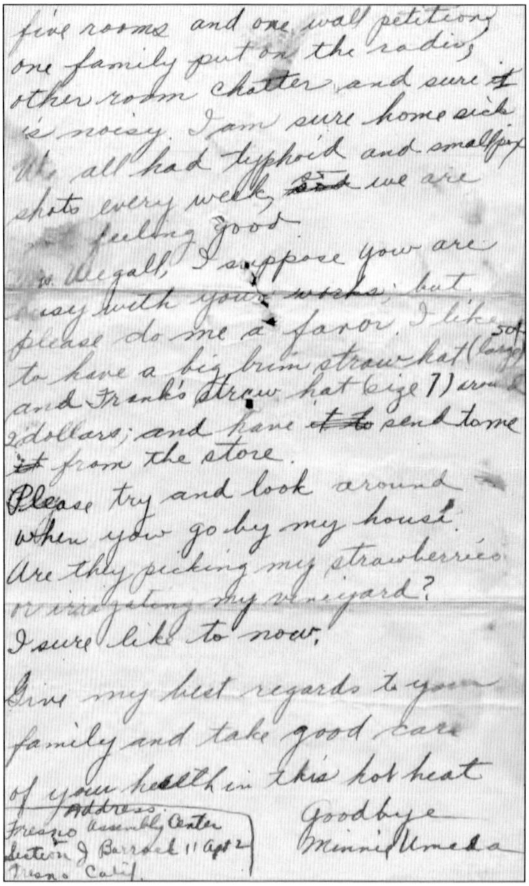

five rooms and one wall petition;
one family put on the radio,
other room chatter and sure it
is noisy. I am sure home sick
We all had typhoid and smallpox
shots every week, we are
feeling good
Mrs. Wegall, I suppose you are
busy with your works, but
please do me a favor. I like
to have a big brim straw hat (large) 50¢
and Frank's straw hat (size 7) around
2 dollars; and have send to me
from the store.
Please try and look around
when you go by my house.
Are they picking my strawberries
or irrigating my vineyard?
I sure like to now.
Give my best regards to your
family and take good care
of your health in this hot heat

Goodbye
Minnie Umeda

Address
Fresno Assembly Center
Western J Barrack 11 Apt 2
Fresno Calif.

Margaret and Henry Waegell of Elk Grove helped to take care of farms while their Japanese American owners were away at concentration camps. This June 8, 1942, letter from Minnie Umeda to Margaret Waegell gives a glimpse of the hot and noisy camp life at Fresno. Minnie Umeda asked for hats in order to avoid the relentless heat of the sun. She also inquired if "they are picking my strawberries or irrigating my vineyard?"

Life carried on behind the barbed-wire fences of the Japanese American concentration camps, including education for all grade levels. A group of high school graduates hailing from 24 different schools, including from the Florin area, make up this June 19, 1942, photograph taken at the Fresno temporary detention center. Note the rows of tarpapered barracks in the background.

Members of the Florin Methodist Church pose in this 1944 photograph at the Jerome incarceration camp. From the preliminary camps called "assembly" centers to the larger long-term camps such as at Jerome, Japanese Americans established religious fellowship groups to continue practicing their faith and to support each other through strong community ties.

Some incarcerated Japanese Americans had the option to leave camp for agricultural work elsewhere. This September 23, 1942, log chronicling Block 207's activities and news for the week reveals that Tom and George Takehara departed Poston concentration camp for work in Idaho. Also noted on the log is an apparent delay in evacuees receiving their pay checks.

Block No. 207 Date 9/23/42

Weather Hot

LOG

I. STAFF

A. Custodian to Post Office

II. BLOCK ACTIVITIES

A. Old Men's softball team lost to 211 team, 13-0 last night at field 207.
B. People of this went to the employment office to send off Tak Urakawa, Tom and George Takehara who left for Idaho.

III. EMERGENCIES: None

IV. VISITORS

A. Timekeeper
B. Press Bulletin runner
C. Express to pick up blankets and baggages of three boys who are leaving for Idaho.

V. MEMORANDUMS

A. From Blk. Mgr. Supvr. requesting 3-4 volunteer parents or school children to clean up barracks and campus of 210.
B. From Blk. Mgr. Supvr. stating that there will be a meeting of chefs, stewards, and representatives of blocks at 214 Mess Hall Sept. 24, 7:30 P. M.
C. From Wade Head, Project Director: Memo on Organization of Div. of Employment.

VI. REMARKS

A. People are still complaining as to when we are to receive lumber for partitions in apartments. Some want more comfortable beds.
B. Several people want their pay-checks on <u>time</u>.

VII. MISCELLANEOUS

A. Two wheelbarrows and 20 bars of soap came in.

VIII. MANAGER'S NOTES

Miyoko Hironaka's family was from Brighton, northwest of Florin. The Hironakas were sent first to the Pinedale temporary detention center and then to the Poston concentration camp in Colorado. Her brother Kuni was sent to Weimar Sanatorium to be treated for tuberculosis and was released in 1945. He was not with his family during their years of incarceration. From left to right are unidentified, Alice Kawabara, Miyoko Hironaka, and unidentified.

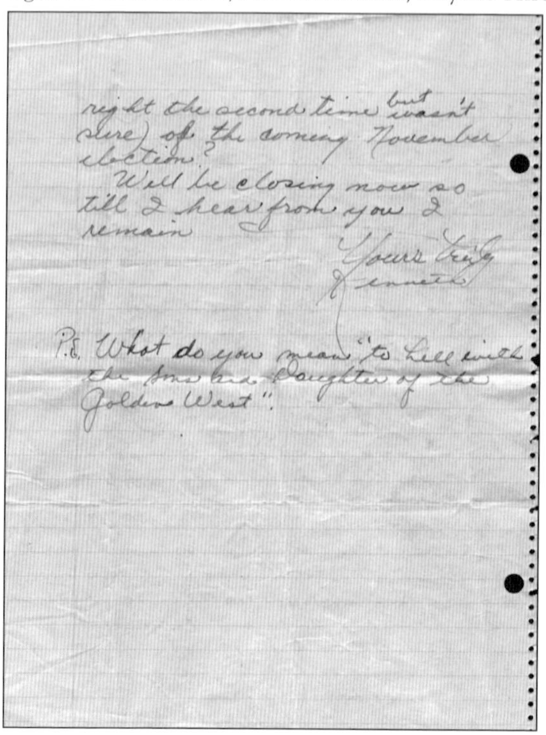

right the second time but wasn't sure) of the coming November election?
Well be closing now so till I hear from you I remain

Yours truly
Kenneth

P.S. What do you mean "to hell with the Sons and Daughter of the Golden West".

At the end of this August 1, 1944, letter, Kenneth Hori asked George Waegell, "What do you mean 'to hell with the Sons and Daughters of the Golden West?' " Perhaps it was because the organization was part of the Japanese Exclusion League of California. The league's aim was to exclude Japanese Americans, and George Waegell's friendship with Hori might have caused him to curse the organization.

This c. 1943 photograph shows an English class at the Poston incarceration camp. Kinue Iwasa (back row, second from right) arrived in Florin as a picture bride in 1915. Her husband, Hisata Iwasa, died in 1942, leaving her to deal not only with his death but the traumatic upheaval of Japanese American forced removal. She and her six children were sent to Poston II incarceration camp.

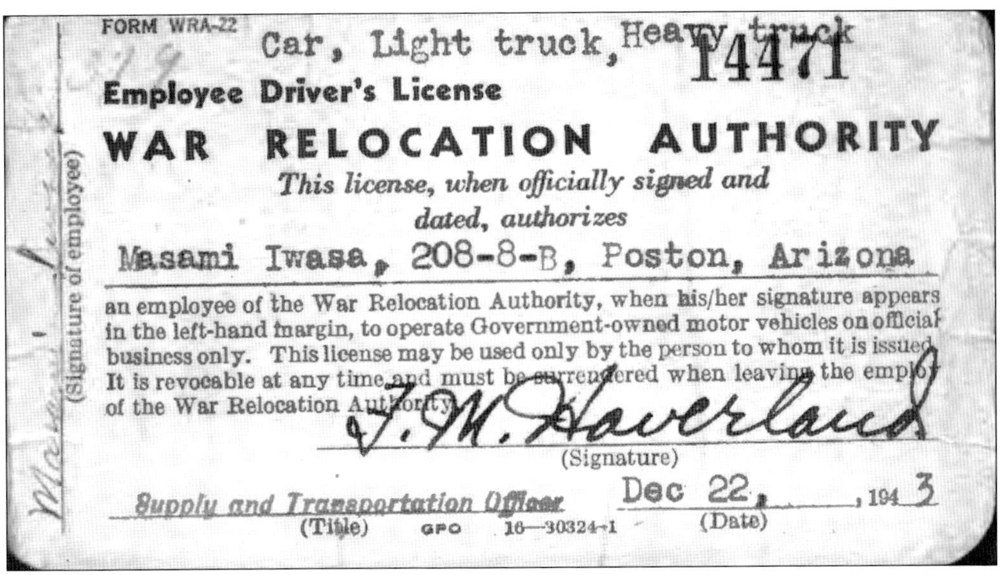

FORM WRA-22 Car, Light truck, Heavy truck T4471

Employee Driver's License

WAR RELOCATION AUTHORITY

This license, when officially signed and dated, authorizes

Masami Iwasa, 208-8-B, Poston, Arizona

an employee of the War Relocation Authority, when his/her signature appears in the left-hand margin, to operate Government-owned motor vehicles on official business only. This license may be used only by the person to whom it is issued. It is revocable at any time and must be surrendered when leaving the employ of the War Relocation Authority.

F. M. Haverland
(Signature)

Supply and Transportation Officer (Title) GPO 16—30324-1 Dec 22, 1943 (Date)

(Signature of employee) Masami Iwasa

Masami Iwasa was granted this War Relocation Authority (WRA) employee driver's license dated December 22, 1943, for use during his detention at the Poston incarceration camp. Japanese American detainees organized and ran the camps' programs, such as schools, food production, and health services. This driver's license allowed Masami Iwasa to drive "government-owned motor vehicles on official business only."

Detainees established activities as a way to maintain structure and a feeling of normalcy in their daily lives. Here is a 1942 photograph of the Florin Pepperettes basketball team at the Fresno "Assembly" Center. Identification is difficult based on notations on the photograph. From left to right are (first row) Nancy Itogawa, unidentified, Clara Sawade, and Lillian Taniguchi; (second row) E.M. Okada, unidentified, Katie Hamataka, Eva Yoshida, and Rosie Tsukamoto.

Members of this championship baseball team wear their respective jerseys from Florin, Taisho YMA (Young Men's Association), Ace Cubs, and San Fernando. The banner reads, "Fresno Assembly Center Champions, Class A, 1942." Continuing their pre-exclusion ability to win championships, the majority of the players wear Florin uniforms.

Pitcher Herb Kurima is holding the championship banner pictured on the previous page in yet another example of Florin's dominance of the sport. Even among the disruption of forced removal, the Florin team continued to win championships. This 1943 photograph was probably taken at the Jerome "Relocation" Center in Arkansas.

Herbert "Moon" Kurima was Florin's star pitcher. As a junior at Elk Grove High School, he pitched the school's first-ever championship game. His parents, Koichi and Tora Kurima, had their own 20-acre strawberry farm on Elder Creek Road. Sadly, Herb's only sister died from the 1918 influenza pandemic. The Kurima family was to suffer another excruciating loss in 1942, but this time it was due to the forced family separation caused by Executive Order 9066. The WCCA denied their disabled brother, Toyoki, from traveling with the rest of the family and instead sent him to an institution. Toyoki, 32 years old at the time of forced removal, was carefully raised and nurtured by his mother, and was familiar only with the Japanese language and Japanese food his mother prepared. Several weeks after the Kurimas were sent to the Fresno "Assembly" Center at the Fresno fairgrounds, the family received news of their beloved Toyoki's death.

Incarcerated Japanese Americans ran the organizations and institutions at the US Army civilian concentration camps in which they were detained. This included schools, churches, hospitals, and as shown in this 1943 photograph, even the fire department. Incarcerated workers were paid extremely low wages for their labor compared to what they would earn in the civilian world. This photograph was taken at the Jerome "Relocation" Center.

A group is standing in front of a fire station in this c. 1943 photograph. Tule Lake Fire Station No. 1 was one of up to four fire stations at the Tule Lake incarceration camp. Nine or ten blocks of barracks made up a ward, and one fire station was responsible for two or three wards.

This undated aerial photograph with a superimposed map gives an overall view of Tule Lake concentration camp's layout and size. A row between blocks of barracks is marked "Fire Break," indicating one of the fire safety measures taken to protect detainees. A hospital, a high school, and the main gate are also noted. According to this map, a guard tower was situated at each "bend in the fence," as noted on one of the labels.

From left to right around 1943, Dr. Taro Akamatsu, Dr. Richards, and Dr. Masayoshi Ito stand together at the Minidoka, Idaho, concentration camp. Dr. Ito administered the inoculation of Florin's Japanese Americans in preparation for being forcibly removed to incarceration camps by the US Army. Married to Shizuko Usami and a graduate of the University of Southern California and La Jolla University, Dr. Ito earned $19 a month as camp doctor.

Yet another disruption awaited some Japanese Americans at the Jerome "Relocation" Center. This c. 1943 photograph shows residents from block 11, barrack 2, room D collecting their belongings in preparation for their move to Rohwer "Relocation" Center, approximately 40 miles away. Some items include a room divider and furniture made by detainees using spare material found at camp.

Isabel Oshiro's brother Capt. George Dakuzaku holds his nephew, a happily smiling Neal Oshiro, in this c. 1943 photograph. After Japanese American exclusion was allowed to lapse, the Oshiros relocated first to Kalamazoo to be with the family of Isabel's sister Mary Tsukamoto. Eventually, the Oshiro family settled in Concord, California, where Isabel and Tom retired with their children Neal and Judy. Neal joined the US Navy and rose to the rank of commander. Judy (Oshiro) Dehont married and raised a family.

Sgt. Kunosake "Kaz" Yoshihata signed this December 3, 1943, photograph for his friend Mary Tsukamoto. He enlisted in the US Army in 1941 when he was 23 years old. Sergeant Yoshihata and three family members, Sokume, Yoshio, and Ishi, were sent to the Fresno temporary detention camp and then to Jerome "Relocation" Center.

The coffin of Cpl. Tadashi Takeuchi of Company C, 100th Battalion, 442 Regimental Combat Team, was delivered to friends and family who waited at the Sacramento train station for its arrival in 1949. Corporal Takeuchi took part in the October 30, 1944, rescue of the Lost Battalion in the Vosges Mountains of France. Corporal Takeuchi posthumously received the Purple Heart and Combat Infantry Badge.

A Purple Heart recipient, S.Sgt. Hirohau Pedro Ouchida (pictured around 1942) fought for the US Army's 442nd Infantry Regiment during World War II. Soldiers of the 442nd were almost all Nisei Japanese Americans. The 442nd suffered the highest casualty rate during the war. After time spent at a veteran's hospital recovering from war wounds, Sergeant Ouchida returned to Florin, where he married Yori Oga and had a son, Peter Kei.

This June 1951 photograph shows Tsune Tahara accepting the Gold Star pin for the loss of her son Corp. Cooper Tahara during a Gold Star ceremony to honor Sacramento and Florin soldiers who died during World War II. Tsune and Kumakichi Tahara's son gave the ultimate sacrifice as a member of the highly decorated 442nd Regiment. The White House letter disclosing this tragic news was delivered to the Taharas while they were detained in a concentration camp in Arkansas. Other mothers who were honored for the valiant actions of their sons in France and Italy included Yoneo Hayashi, Tsuru Nakagaki, Asa Abe, Tane Akiyama, and Tsuneo Sakai. James Takeuchi received the medal on behalf of the Takeuchi family. The ceremony, which took place at Sacramento's Fox Senator Theater, was followed by a screening of *Go for Broke!*, a film about Japanese American soldiers who fought in World War II.

George Inouye and Frank Oshita stand guard as Tane Akiyama mourns her son Zentaro (George) Akiyama at his funeral in this 1944 photograph. George Akiyama was killed at the Battle of Hill No. 140 in Castellino, Italy, on July 3, 1944. He was a Nisei soldier in the famed 442nd Regiment, Company F. Tane Akiyama was also present at the 1951 Gold Star ceremony shown on the previous page.

World War II claimed the lives of all three servicemen in this c. 1943 photograph. From left to right are Abraham Ohama, Kaz Masuda, and Zentaro (George) Akiyama. Tane Akiyama received her Gold Star pin in the 1951 ceremony in Sacramento. Abraham Ohama died in Bruyeres, France, and was posthumously awarded a Silver Star medal.

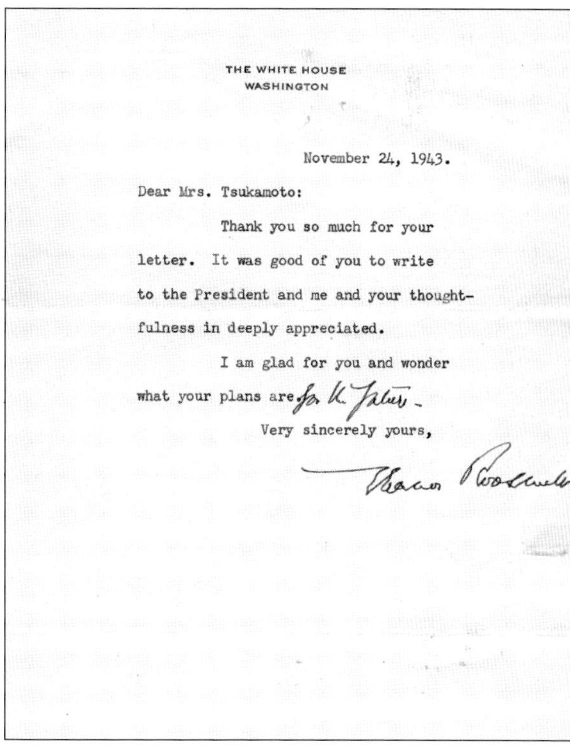

THE WHITE HOUSE
WASHINGTON

November 24, 1943.

Dear Mrs. Tsukamoto:

Thank you so much for your letter. It was good of you to write to the President and me and your thoughtfulness in deeply appreciated.

I am glad for you and wonder what your plans are for the future.

Very sincerely yours,

Eleanor Roosevelt

Mary Tsukamoto had written to First Lady Eleanor Roosevelt and was excited to receive a letter in return. The letter, typed on White House stationery, is dated November 24, 1943, but Mary didn't receive it until the following January while she and her family were held in the Jerome concentration camp. The majority of the letter is typed except for the last three words "for the future" and Eleanor Roosevelt's signature.

Julia Dakuzaku, Mary Tsukamoto's youngest sister, stands in her Women's Army Corps uniform on February 19, 1945. Julia worked at the Peter Pan Bakery in Kalamazoo after the exclusion order was allowed to lapse. She was fired when she refused to go back to night shifts after white customers boycotted the bakery for allowing a Japanese American at the front counter. Julia subsequently joined the Women's Army Corps, seeking her own path after the racism and rejection she endured during mass incarceration of Japanese Americans. In response to a care package from Mary, Julia wrote, "I am anxious to come home to Florin in a few days." These were the last words Julia's family received from her. Tragically, Julia Dakuzaku took her own life in September 1945 and was sent home in an American flag–covered casket. She received a military funeral.

Five

Years of the Pine

The caption written on this 1945 photograph reads, "Home again! Shopping in Sacramento." After their time at the Fresno "Assembly" Center and Jerome concentration camp, Al, Mary, and Marielle Tsukamoto moved to Kalamazoo, Michigan, in November 1943. The family returned to Florin on July 10, 1945, but was not prepared for the devastating changes that had occurred in such a short time.

Family history states that the Kawadas left Florin around 1910 to avoid dealing with destructive flooding, and this 1959 photograph shows Choji and Mitsuye Kawada on their celery farm in West Sacramento after World War II. Despite the disruption of their forced removal to Japanese American concentration camps in 1942, the Kawadas returned to their lifelong vocation of farming.

From Florin to Tule Lake to West Sacramento, Choji and Mitsuye Kawada and their family overcame the kind of adversity that would derail many others. The family, including Barney, Charles, Alice, William, and Shigeru, was incarcerated at the Tule Lake Japanese American concentration camp.

Early American immigration legislation denied Chinese and Japanese immigrants the ability to naturalize. The Issei in this 1954 graduation photograph finally earned their long-overdue citizen status due to the 1952 passage of the Immigration and Nationality Act. The Florin Japanese American Citizens League organized naturalization classes such as this one, taught by Mr. Fujimori, that included Tsune and Kumakichi Tahara and Kuzo Tsukamoto.

Friends gather to celebrate Sadaichi Okimura's 73rd birthday in this c. 1950 photograph. From left to right are Reverend Tsumura, Makiyo Okimura, Sadaichi Okimura, Kuzo Tsukamoto, and Shonosuke Kushi. Shonosuke Kushi and his wife, Masa, owned a farm at Stockton Boulevard and Gerber Road. The Kushis, with their two children Lily and Misu, were removed to Tule Lake and then the Jerome concentration camp. The family returned to Sacramento in the early 1950s, a number of years after Japanese exclusion was allowed to lapse.

Florin's baseball teams won a number of Rural League championships before World War II. In fact, they continued to come out on top even during detention in Japanese American incarceration camps. This 1949 team photograph shows that Florin's winning trend continued when players returned to Florin after the exclusion order was no longer enforced and Japanese Americans were released from detention.

Emmie Takehara poses with a toddler on her knee outside her and her husband Paul Takehara's Walsh Station store in this c. 1950 photograph. Paul Takehara opened the store in 1946 after he was discharged from the US Army. The store was at the corner of Jackson and Bradshaw Roads.

Mary and daughter Marielle Tsukamoto stand together on the left, Kame Dakuzaku is at center, and Kuzo Tsukamoto stands second from the right in this June 23, 1945, photograph taken in Kalamazoo. Mary's husband, Al Tsukamoto, found work at Peter Pan Bakery in Kalamazoo before the Jerome concentration camp closed. Camp officials recruited the bakery to hire newly freed Japanese Americans. By the spring of 1944, Kuzo, Mary's brother George, and her sister Julia were all hired for night work at the bakery. Customers boycotted the business when Julia was allowed to work at the front counter.

Some members of the Tsukamoto family pose in front of their house at 410 West Dutton Street in Kalamazoo in 1945. Daughter Marielle's school was only a block away, and stores and a church were also nearby. For Mary Tsukamoto, the adjustment to having freedom once again was a challenging but happy transition, and the local Parent Teacher Association and Young Women's Christian Association provided a supportive community.

This c. 1950 photograph shows grandmother Ito Tsukamoto, granddaughter Marielle Tsukamoto, and grandson Harold Ouchida Jr., whose mother was Edith (Tsukamoto) Ouchida digging a hole, most likely for the gas pump behind them. Four generations of the Ouchida family have lived in Florin, beginning with Issei Sennosuke and Soyo Ouchida from Fukuoka Prefecture.

Kuzo and Ito Tsukamoto married in 1896 in Hiroshima, Japan, where they were both born. They are pictured here celebrating their 50th anniversary in 1946 surrounded by family members. Identified are Al Tsukamoto; Mary Tsukamoto; Marielle Tsukamoto; Nami Tsukamoto; Edith Ouchida; Harold Ouchida with his and Edith's children Lucille, Ken, Earl, Lester, and Sammy; Hiro Ouchida; Raymond and Violet Ogata; Charlie Ogata; Ito Tsukamoto; and Kuzo Tsukamoto.

The closing of detention centers often separated Japanese American family members in their search for new beginnings. This 1949 Nakano family photograph was taken in Seabrook, New Jersey, after their release from the Manzanar concentration camp. A leading frozen and canned food producer, Seabrook Farms hired many Japanese Americans beginning around 1944. From left to right are (first row) Walter, Eleanor, Carolyn, and Matsumura; (second row) Fred, Ruby (Uchida), and Grace.

Matriarch Shizu Uchida spends time with one of her daughters, Ruby Nakano, and grandsons Jeffrey and Douglas Nakano in this undated photograph. Issei and many Nisei Japanese Americans were reluctant to discuss the experience of forced removal and incarceration for the trauma of racism and shame of being "otherized" from what it means to be American.

Taken in 1955, this photograph captures a tender moment between Shige Kiino and her swaddled granddaughter Diane Kiino at their house in Kalamazoo. Shige Kiino was the first Issei woman to arrive in Florin in 1900, and lived to 104 years of age.

Bibliography

California Digital Newspaper Collection. cdnc.ucr.edu

Dedication Book Committee. *Oneness: Dedication of the Florin Buddhist Temple, 1976*. Florin, CA: Florin Buddhist Temple, 1977.

Densho. densho.org, encyclopedia.densho.org

Florin Area Reunion III Committee. *Florin Area Recollections: Southern California Florin Area Reunion*. 1988.

Florin Homecoming Reunion Committee. *II Florin Area Reunion: Pre-evacuation Japanese Community Region [of] Florin, Elk Grove, Mayhew, Perkins, Taishoku, Brighton*. 1986.

Florin Historical Society. *Once-in-a-Lifetime-Reunion, Florin, California*. 1985.

Florin JACL. florinjacl.com

Heizer, Robert F. and Alan J. Almquist. *The Other Californians: Prejudice and Discrimination under Spain, Mexico, and the United States to 1920*. Berkeley, CA: University of California Press, 1971.

"How the Japanese Grow Strawberries in Florin." *Pacific Rural Press*, February 4, 1905. California Digital Newspaper Collection. Accessed February 18, 2020.

Okimoto, Ruth Y. *Sharing a Desert Home: Life on the Colorado Indian Reservation, Poston, Arizona, 1942–1945*. California Civil Liberties Public Education Program. Special Report of *News from Native California*. Berkeley, CA: Malcolm Margolin, 2001.

Pinkerton, Elizabeth. *History Happened Here Book I: River, Oaks, Gold*. Elk Grove, CA: Laguna Publishers, 2000.

———. *History Happened Here Book II: Fields, Farms, Schools*. Elk Grove, CA: Laguna Publishers, 2002.

Sato, Kiyo. *Kiyo's Story: A Japanese American Family's Quest for the American Dream*. New York, NY: Soho Press, 2009.

Starr, Kevin. *California: A History*. New York, NY: Modern Library, 2005.

Tsukamoto, Marielle, Twila Tomita, et al. *Florin JACL 75th Anniversary: 1935–2010. Strength through Unity*. 2010.

Tsukamoto, Mary, and Elizabeth Pinkerton. *We the People: A Story of Internment in America*. Elk Grove, CA: Laguna Publishers, 1987.

Wildie, Kevin. *Sacramento's Historic Japantown: Legacy of a Lost Neighborhood*. Charleston, SC: History Press, 2013.

Discover Thousands of Local History Books Featuring Millions of Vintage Images

Arcadia Publishing, the leading local history publisher in the United States, is committed to making history accessible and meaningful through publishing books that celebrate and preserve the heritage of America's people and places.

Find more books like this at
www.arcadiapublishing.com

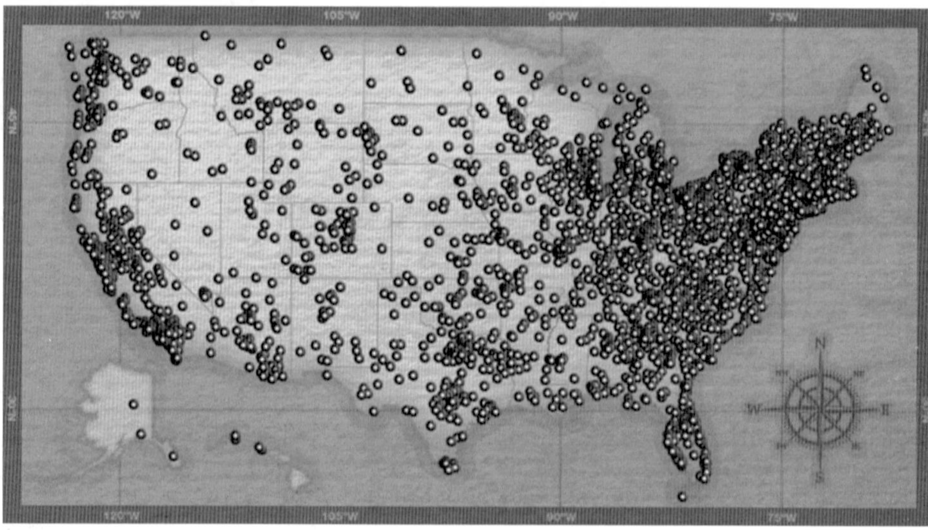

Search for your hometown history, your old stomping grounds, and even your favorite sports team.

Consistent with our mission to preserve history on a local level, this book was printed in South Carolina on American-made paper and manufactured entirely in the United States. Products carrying the accredited Forest Stewardship Council (FSC) label are printed on 100 percent FSC-certified paper.

MADE IN THE USA